FINDING PEACE IN TROUBLED WATERS

FINDING PEACE IN TROUBLED WATERS

1 0   L I F E   P R E S E R V E R S

FOR WHEN YOUR SHIP SPRINGS A LEAK

ART E. BERG

Deseret Book Company
Salt Lake City, Utah

Library of Congress Cataloging-in-Publication Data

Berg, Art E.
   Finding peace in troubled waters : ten life preservers for when your ship springs a leak / Art E. Berg.
      p.   cm.
   Includes bibliographical references and index.
   ISBN 1-57345-047-2
   1. Berg, Art E.—Health. 2. Quadriplegics—United States— Biography. 3. Physically handicapped. 4. Adjustment (Psychology)
I. Title.
RC406.Q33B474   1995
362.4'3'092—dc20   95-24242
[b]   CIP

Printed in the United States of America

10   9   8   7   6   5   4   3   2   1

To the three men
who threw me these life preservers
when I needed them most:

My father-in-law,
Ken Howard,
who taught me the power
of incrementalism

My mission president,
Morris Q. Bastian,
who put me on the
"road less traveled"

And most of all
to my biggest hero, my father,
Dave Berg,
who never gave up on me.

Thank you for saving my life.

"This is a tremendous book for all seasons. Whether your ship has recently struck an iceberg or is still tied up at the dock waiting to sail, you will find rich understanding of life's troubled times in Art Berg's new release. And it would be a terrific gift to a friend in need of clarity and peace."

—Taylor Hartman, Ph.D., *The Color Code*

"Life has no guarantees. Just as a large ocean liner needs life preservers, we need to have already in place, before a crisis hits, ideas and concepts that will help us get through even the most difficult of life's challenges. *Finding Peace* provides us with these ideas and does it in a delightfully entertaining manner. Art Berg is truly a marvel!"

—Jack Weyland, *On the Run*

Contents

Acknowledgments

There are many people to thank when a project such as this book has finally been completed. Many of the life preservers I share in these pages have been taught to me and reinforced by those I love.

To name a few, a special thanks to the following family and friends: Dave and Betty Berg, Ken and Rae Howard, Paul and Dawnie Berg, Carla and Richard Bischoff, Beverly and Wade Robison, Mike Berg, Roger Berg, Martha Jorgensen, Todd and Rachel Humphrey, Scott and Cassie Howard, Mike Howard, Brent and Margaret Yorgason, Brad and Debi Wilcox, John Bytheway, Stephen Covey, Anthony Robbins, Jack Weyland, Morris Q. and Elaine Bastian, R. Perry and Pauline Greenwood, Taylor Hartman, Steve and Julie Lemmon, Dan and Karen Pedersen, Mitch and Annette Scott, Karalynn Waldon, Matt and Tiffany Judd, Ted and Deborah Peck, Darryl Fry, Chris Yondow,

Sharlene Wells Hawkes, and the countless others who have influenced and blessed my life.

I also would like to especially thank my wife, Dallas, for her undying love and faith in me. And to our children, McKenzie and Dalton, for teaching me every day what love really is.

Finally, a special thanks to Sheri Dew, Suzanne Brady, Kent Ware, and the entire staff of Deseret Book for their efforts and enthusiasm in bringing this book to life.

Introduction

Pain, frustration, and discouragement are a natural part of life, but too often we permit these negative elements to rob us of our sense of peace—and I believe that only then have we truly lost something. Once, while the Savior and his disciples were aboard a ship, "there arose a great storm of wind, and the waves beat into the ship, so that it was now full." The disciples trembled with fear, certain of their impending doom, as Jesus slept. Fear overcame their faith, and the disciples awoke the Savior, "Master, carest thou not that we perish? And he arose, and rebuked the wind, and said unto the sea, Peace, be still. And the wind ceased, and there was a great calm" (Mark 4:37-39).

Regardless of the storms of our lives, despite the winds that blow and the waves that beat us, the message of the Savior's life is simple and clear: we can still enjoy a full measure of peace in our lives and receive comfort to our souls. Even while weathering the most violent storms, we can still sleep. And though our ship may be taking on water, we need not be alarmed. There are life preservers that bring the promise of peace and survival even amid the storms of life. Those life preservers do not protect against the craggy shores and treacherous shoals of life. They do not promise a life free from worry, pain, or setbacks. But when our ship begins to take on water, as it will from time to time, we have something to hold on to, and we can find peace.

The *Titanic*

I awoke with a sudden jolt to the sound of twisting metal and breaking glass. Then suddenly it was quiet again. Opening my eyes, I found my whole world was darkness. I could feel the warmth of blood covering my face. And then the pain. It was becoming excruciating and overwhelming. I could hear voices calling my name as I slipped away again into unconsciousness.

At the age of nearly twenty-one, I had completed my mission, and I was happier than I had ever been in my life. I was a competitive water-skier. I snow skied, played golf, tennis, racquetball, basketball, and volleyball. I bowled in a league. I ran nearly every day. I had just started a tennis court construction company, and so my financial future looked exciting and bright. And I was engaged to the most beautiful woman in the world. Then a tragedy occurred—or, at least, some called it that.

Saying good-bye to my family in California on a beautiful Christmas evening, I left for Utah with a friend. I was going to spend the rest of the holidays with my fiancée, Dallas. We were to finish the plans for our wedding, which was to take place in five short weeks. I drove for the first eight hours of the trip, and then I traded places with my friend, who had been resting. I climbed into the passenger's seat, fastened my seat belt, and went to sleep while my friend drove into the darkness. An hour and a half later, he fell asleep at the wheel. The car hit a cement abutment, went up and over it, and rolled a number of times.

The car finally came to a stop, but I wasn't in it. Ejected from the vehicle, I had broken my neck on the desert floor. I was paralyzed from the chest down. After I arrived by ambulance at a hospital in Las Vegas, Nevada, a doctor told me I had become a quadriplegic. I had lost the use of my feet and legs. I had lost the use of my stomach muscles and two of three major chest muscles. I had lost the use of my right triceps. I had lost most of the use of my shoulders and arms. And I had lost all use of my hands.

The doctors said I would have to learn to dream new dreams and think new thoughts. They said I would never work again—I was pretty excited about that one—because 93 percent of persons in my condition never did. They told me that I would never drive again, that for the rest of my life I would be completely dependent on others to help me eat, get dressed, and move from place to place. They said I should not expect to get married because . . . who would want me? They said I would never again play in any sport or competitive activity.

For the first time in my life, I was really afraid. I was afraid that what they were saying might really be true.

Pain Hurts in Any Form

As I have traveled the world since that day, sharing a message of encouragement and hope, many people have shared with me their own struggles, challenges, and obstacles in life. Many of these people preface their own experiences with, "Of course, my experiences were nothing like yours." What they mean to imply is that their experiences weren't as difficult, tragic, or as painful as mine. I take issue with that.

If I have learned anything in the years since my accident, it is this: pain hurts in any form. My pain is no greater than that of a mother who has lost a wayward child to alcohol and drugs. My heartache is no deeper than that of a parent who is having a difficult time financially supporting a family. And my tears are no wetter than those of a young person who has lost sight of all hopes and dreams and wonders what tomorrow will bring.

In his book *The Road Less Traveled,* M. Scott Peck states: "Life is difficult. This is a great truth. Perhaps the greatest of all the truths. Because once we understand it, then we can transcend it." Once we truly know that life is difficult and accept that fact, then it no longer matters. Peck explains further, "Most do not fully see this truth that life is difficult. Instead they moan more or less incessantly, noisily, or subtly, about the enormity of their problems, their burdens, and their difficulties as if life were generally easy, as if life *should* be easy."

If you have not experienced such difficulty yet, then I can promise that one day it will come. The nature of life is that we will all experience the kind of pain, frustration, and even tragedy

5

that will make us want to quit, give up, or give in. It may be the struggling of one of our children who may have made some bad choices. It could be unexpected illness or accident. Perhaps it is the unrelenting stress of daily responsibilities, mounting debt, or unresolved conflicts.

This Is Not a Chance World

Many years ago I read an unusual book entitled *A Chance World.* In that fictitious world nothing was certain. In the morning you never knew if the sun or the moon and stars would come up. You weren't sure if rainwater or cats and dogs would fall from the skies. If you planted an apple seed, you had to wait to see if you would get apples or oranges or pears or nothing at all. Seasons of the year randomly came and went. Nobody knew when to plant or when to harvest. And so no one did anything at all. In that world, you couldn't count on anything. Knowledge had little value because it never stayed the same. There was no truth.

Fortunately, you and I do not live in a world of chance. We live in a world that is created, organized, and governed by laws—laws we can count on and live by.

The Savior taught, "And ye shall know the truth, and the truth shall make you free" (John 8:32). Free from what? Truth is knowledge that was true yesterday and remains true today and tomorrow—it never changes. Ignorance of the truth does not change its consequences. For example, it is a truth that water freezes at 32 degrees Fahrenheit. That is true today, it was true in Adam's day, and it will be true tomorrow. If a young man bought a one-hundred-thousand-dollar car and drove it into the tops of the mountains in the dead of winter without benefit of antifreeze, his car's engine would be destroyed—even if he had never been taught the truth and the consequences of the fact that water freezes at 32 degrees Fahrenheit.

On the other hand, by learning, understanding, and obeying that truth, we inherit the blessings that naturally follow. If the young car owner had learned the truth, understood it, and obeyed it, he would still be enjoying his expensive car. On a grander scale, the discovery of the truth that water boils at 212 degrees Fahrenheit and creates steam at that temperature made possible the development of the railroad locomotive, enabling tons of steel to be moved across America.

So how does all this relate to the individual who, because of the storms of life, has lost his sense of peace? Simple. There are laws that govern peace, despite the circumstances, environment, or condition of our lives. When we learn, understand, and obey those laws, we inherit the natural consequences of obedience to them— namely, peace. When we obey those laws, no one and nothing can take the peace from our hearts. The Lord has declared, "I, the Lord, am bound when ye do what I say; but when ye do not what I say, ye have no promise" (D&C 82:10). God, too, is governed by law. The Savior came to teach us truth, and what he taught two thousand years ago remains true today. It will set us free.

The Life Preservers of Peace

In April 1912, the *Titanic* set sail from England for America.

7

It was a ship thought to be so technologically advanced, so masterfully crafted, that no sea could overcome its awesome power. It was said to be a "lifeboat unto itself." Because of that belief the ship had an inadequate number of lifeboats on board. That false belief cost fifteen hundred people their lives in the icy waters of the Atlantic when an iceberg ripped through inches of steel and exposed the vulnerability of the mightiest ship of all.

We can search the world for stronger emotional steel for our lives. We can attempt to find better ways to insulate ourselves against the cold waters of life through self-improvement gurus, subliminal tapes, and best-selling books. We can desperately seek the advanced technologies of personal development. And yet none of these can stop the icy waters from inevitably rushing into our hearts and lives as we find ourselves scrambling for some form of life preserver . . . only to discover we didn't take any with us.

After I broke my neck I scrambled about as my ship took on water faster than I could ever have imagined. Fortunately, when the icy waters of pain and discouragement reached me and my world was dark and all appeared to be lost, I reached out and found a life preserver to hold on to. I found more than one. I found truths that have brought me peace. Now I offer them to you. Whether your ship is sailing upon calm waters or is heading for uncharted seas or you are struggling to keep your head above the crashing waves, I am throwing these life preservers of truth to you with one suggestion: Hold on . . . Peace, be still.

Dreams Are Never Destroyed by Circumstances

O ur dreams, hopes, and aspirations are the essence of life. They give us courage and will. They feed, motivate, and inspire us to take risks, move forward, and meet our daily challenges. Our dreams are life preservers when the storms rage.

In his book *Man's Search for Meaning* (New York: Washington Square Press, 1985), Viktor Frankl describes the horrors he endured while imprisoned in a Nazi concentration camp during World War II. He suffered through atrocities that you and I could not even imagine. Because he was Jewish, they tortured his body, murdered his wife, and slaughtered his children. After enduring years of mental, physical, and emotional torture, he was finally liberated.

While suffering under those dire conditions, Victor Frankl, a psychologist with years of training, observed the difference between those who survived and those who did not. Perhaps his most profound discovery was that those who continued to hold tightly to their hopes and dreams, despite their circumstances, were able to find purpose in their suffering. By so doing, they tapped into hidden reservoirs of strength and developed increased capacity to endure.

It is a natural response, when faced with discouraging circumstances, to conclude that we will never realize our dreams. We sometimes feel overwhelmed by hopelessness. When I was struggling to find meaning during those first few hours and days after my accident, I was repeatedly cautioned by my doctor to keep my expectations low. I was warned against the alleged dangers of harboring a sense of false hope.

I do not believe in false hope. I only believe in false hopelessness. For all medicine knows today, I believe there is more we do not know. Hope is the fuel of dreams. Hope is the brother of faith and the strength for tomorrow. Dreams are born in the heart and mind, and only there can they ever die.

Tomorrow Will Be Better

Lying in that hospital bed in Las Vegas, I wondered where all my hopes and dreams had gone. I wondered if I would ever be made whole again. I wondered if I would work, get married, have a family, and enjoy any of the activities of life that had previously brought me such joy.

During this critical time of natural doubts and fears, when my whole world seemed so dark, my mother came to my bedside and whispered in my ear, "Art, while the difficult takes time, the impossible just takes a little longer." Suddenly a once-darkened

10

room filled with the light of hope and faith that tomorrow would be better.

I have since become president of my own company. I am a professional speaker and a published author. I travel more than two hundred thousand miles a year to share the message of *The Impossible Just Takes a Little Longer*™ with Fortune 500 companies, national associations, sales organizations, and youth groups with some audiences exceeding sixty thousand people. In 1992, I was named the Young Entrepreneur of the Year for a six-state region by the Small Business Administration. In 1994, *Success* magazine honored me as one of the Great Comebacks of the Year. These are dreams that have come true for me. They came true, not in spite of my circumstances, but, perhaps, because of them.

I have learned to drive again—a dangerous thing for a quadriplegic. I go where I want to go; I do what I want to do. I am completely independent, and I take care of myself. Since that day, some feeling has returned to my body, and I have received back some of the use of my right triceps.

A year and a half after that fateful day, I was married to the same beautiful and wonderful young woman I had originally planned to marry. In 1992, Dallas, my wife, was named Mrs. Utah and was third runner-up to Mrs. USA. (We didn't win the boat!) And we have two children—a daughter named McKenzie Raeanne and a son named Dalton Arthur—who are the joys of our lives.

I have also returned to the world of sports. I have learned to swim, scuba dive, and parasail. (I believe I am the first quadriplegic of record to parasail.) I have learned to snow ski. I have also learned to play full-contact rugby. (How could I get hurt any worse?) I also race wheelchairs in 10Ks and marathons. On 10 July 1993, I became the first quadriplegic in the world to race 325 miles in seven days between Salt Lake City and St. George, Utah—probably not one of the brightest things I have ever done, but certainly one of the most difficult.

Why have I done all of these things? Because a long time ago I chose to listen to the voice of my mother and to my heart rather than to the cascading chorus of dissenting voices around me that included skeptical medical professionals. I decided that my then current circumstances did not mean I had to let go of my dreams. I found a reason to hope again.

Adversity Draws Us Closer to Our Dreams

I went through some particularly difficult times when I was sixteen and seventeen. It was as though I was living two lives. One side of me attended early-morning seminary for four years, rarely missing a day. I was among the fastest scripture-chasers in the region. I attended all of my church meetings on Sunday and activities during the week. I dressed for Sunday in a three-piece black suit, trying to set a higher standard for other young priesthood holders. I anticipated and eagerly looked forward to serving a two-year mission for the Lord. My hair was always cut short, and I dressed well. I never experimented with drugs or used alcohol or tobacco. And I maintained moral standards. So, what was wrong?

In my other life, I defied authority. I became frequently delinquent from school. I developed an attitude that created many situations in which I chose to defend myself physically. I lived life dangerously with a foolish sense of immortality. I had as many enemies as I had friends. At the depths of my personal despair, I was kicked out of my high school and told that I could never return. Worst of all, I was very unhappy.

I didn't like who or what I was. I was struggling to identify with something. I had sunk to the bottom.

Then I began to reach out. I reached to God as I never had done before in my life. I reached to my family, and I found that that was where my best friends really were. I reached to the scriptures and the prophets to find reservoirs of truth that would set me free. And I reached to the bookshelves to find new meaning in life.

I made many great discoveries during that learning process. Among them was a truth that I did not learn the real power of for years to come. I developed a belief that nothing bad happens in a person's life without an equal or greater benefit coming in return. I gained the understanding that pain will do only one of two things—either it will push us to the furthest point from our dreams or it will draw us closer to them than any other circumstance could. The choice is ours.

Take Thomas Edison, for example. He "devoted ten years and all of his money to developing the nickel alkaline storage battery at a time when he was almost penniless. Through that period of time, his record and film production company was supporting the storage battery effort. Then one night the terrifying cry of 'Fire!'

echoed through the film plant. Spontaneous combustion had ignited some chemicals. Within moments all of the packing compounds, celluloid for records, film, and other flammable goods had gone up in flames. Fire companies from eight towns arrived, but the heat was so intense and the water pressure so low that the fire hoses had no effect. Edison was sixty-seven years old—no age to begin anew. His daughter was frantic, wondering if he was safe, if his spirit was broken, how he would handle a crisis such as this at his age. She saw him running toward her. He spoke first. He said, 'Where's your mother? Go get her. Tell her to get her friends. They'll never see another fire like this as long as they live!' At five-thirty the next morning, with the fire barely under control, he called his employees together and announced, 'We're rebuilding.' One man was told to lease all the machine shops in the area, another to obtain a wrecking crane from the Erie Railroad Company. Then, almost as an afterthought, Edison added, 'Oh, by the way. Anybody know where we can get some money?'

"Virtually everything we now recognize as a Thomas Edison contribution to our lives came *after* that disaster" (Jeffrey R. Holland, *However Long and Hard the Road* [Salt Lake City: Deseret Book, 1989], pp. 3–4).

Out of the pain of my teenage years, I began to lay the foundation of testimony and belief that would serve me well through a successful mission in the Rapid City South Dakota Mission. When I broke my neck on a desert floor the very foundation of my life shook until I thought it would crumble—but it stood.

14

What If the Lamanites Had Never Come

After being threatened by King Noah and his wicked priests, Alma left with his followers to establish their own community, but the Lord warned them that the armies of the Lamanites would come upon them if they did not flee again. Alma and his followers again uprooted themselves and fled for eight days into the wilderness, until they "came to a land, yea, even a very beautiful and pleasant land, a land of pure water" (Mosiah 23:4).

Alma and his people tilled the soil, organized themselves, and built buildings. In time they established a city and called it Helam. Enjoying the natural consequences of their righteous and industrious lives, the people prospered. I am sure that many expected that to be the end of their struggles, that they would live happily ever after.

The very opposite happened. After nearly twenty-four years, while the people were working in their fields, an army of Lamanites—their mortal enemies—literally stumbled upon them. The Lamanites had become lost from their own city and were trying desperately to find their way home again.

Why? Why did the Lamanites have to get lost? Why, after the sacrifices Alma's people had made to build a city where they could worship their God, teach their children, and enjoy peace, did their enemies have to discover them? Why didn't God protect them? Why didn't he intervene in their behalf and lead the Lamanites away from them? Hadn't they lived the gospel? Weren't they true to their covenants? Weren't their desires righteous?

The people of the city of Helam were frightened and ran to

confer with their high priest and leader, Alma. He counseled his followers to pray to God for deliverance. The Lamanites' hearts were softened, and they spared their lives.

But the Lamanites did take military control of the city. One of the wicked priests of King Noah was declared king, and "he exercised authority over them, and put tasks upon them, and put taskmasters over them" (Mosiah 24:9). So great were the afflictions upon the people that they cried mightily to the Lord. Threatening them with death, the king commanded them to stop their cries.

"And Alma and his people did not raise their voices to the Lord their God, but did pour out their hearts to him; and he did know the thoughts of their hearts" (Mosiah 24:12). The Lord eased the burdens upon his people's backs as a witness that he does visit his children in the midst of their afflictions.

Then, making good on his promise, the Lord caused that a deep sleep should come upon the Lamanites, and Alma and his people fled again into the wilderness. While they were stopped to give thanks for their deliverance, the Lord warned them that the Lamanites were in pursuit, and Alma's people continued their exodus in haste. After twelve days, they came upon the city of Zarahemla, where they were received by King Mosiah "with joy" (v. 25).

What a miracle! Who would have thought? Alma and his followers were brought to the great city of Zarahemla and became united with a people of like mind, heart, and desires. To answer the question, Why did the Lord allow the Lamanites to get lost?

16

it is necessary to ask another one: If the Lamanites had never come, would Alma and his people ever have found Zarahemla? Alma's followers found Zarahemla not in spite of the Lamanites but perhaps because of them.

What Would You Trade?

Some years ago I was in a business relationship that became an enormous burden. I felt trapped and used. I felt cheated by the other parties. I felt I had been treated dishonorably, and it was costing me financially and emotionally.

Before long, attorneys were introduced into the embroiled relationship. Hurtful words were spoken, threats were made, and battle plans were detailed for a lengthy legal confrontation. I felt my world spinning out of control. Tens of thousands of dollars were being spent to keep the legal wheels turning. Time was taken from other interests and needs, and money was being consumed in a skirmish of pride.

Why? I thought I was doing what was right. I was keeping my covenants with the Lord. I had tried to serve others, be honest, and give of myself. At the time, I was speaking about three times a week at Church firesides, youth programs, and high schools—all on my own time because I wanted to make a difference. I was having trouble understanding why this other part of my life was coming apart at the seams. Despite my strong belief that "nothing bad ever happens without an equal or greater benefit coming in return," I was struggling to keep my hopes and dreams alive.

Then, late one night, I got a phone call from my attorney.

17

Thinking he was calling about an upcoming legal deposition, I was surprised when he asked me, "Art, have you and Dallas considered adopting any children?" I was taken aback. I responded that we had discussed it but had decided against it because of the time, money, and stress involved in such a pursuit. I told him that we had concluded to spend our efforts in a continuing attempt to bear our own children, despite our having tried unsuccessfully for two years.

Not easily discouraged, my attorney explained that aside from his specialty as a business attorney, he also had done a number of adoptions. Acknowledging that we had never approached him with the intention of adopting, he told me that a situation had arisen in which a fifteen-month-old girl was available for adoption. He had a list of potential parents who were on a waiting list, but he said he felt spiritually compelled to call us and at least offer her to our family. Dallas and I were shocked, to say the least. Within forty-eight hours, our new daughter, McKenzie, came home—to our home!

I cannot express what joy she has brought into our lives in the years she has been with us. I cannot even fathom what our lives would be like without her. Dallas and I have felt from the moment we said yes that McKenzie had always been meant for our family—she just had to take a different route to get there.

Within just a few months, the legal battle I was in came to an end. The question is, If the painful legal confrontation had never commenced, would McKenzie ever have found her way to our home? I believe that we have been blessed by McKenzie's life forever, not in spite of the legal fight but perhaps because of it.

Yet Learned He Obedience

When we suffer from discouragement, frustration, and pain, it becomes easy to let go of our dreams. When we surrender our hopes to our circumstances, they become our master. I am not suggesting we should hold to unrealistic dreams or expectations, but at the same time, I am saying that when we hold onto even simple ambition through the storms of life, it will bring strength, courage, and even peace. Our dreams ignite hope, our hope inspires will, our will fosters confidence, and our confidence rewards us with peace.

The apostle Paul, writing of the Savior's experiences, said, "Yet learned he obedience by the things which he suffered" (Hebrews 5:8). Jesus Christ became the Savior of the world, not in spite of his sufferings, but perhaps because of them.

If you are struggling, if you are battling the crashing waves of life, if you wonder how long you can survive, then I am throwing you this life preserver from my own experience: do not give up on your dreams. Dreams should never be destroyed by circumstances. Dreams are born in the heart and mind, and only there can they ever die.

The Question of the Ages

The lights from above burned my eyes. Everything was blurry, but I was aware that people were rushing from one side of me to the other. Voices spoke in urgent tones, though I could not make out what they were talking about. I could feel a heavy weight pulling on my head and the cold metal tongs embedded in my scalp that held it. The skin from my nose was being tugged at as someone worked to stitch my wounds.

Where was I? What was happening? My mind raced for answers. Somehow, I knew I was hurt really bad. Why me? Why now? Why . . . ? The salt from my tears stung my face as I drifted away again.

From the beginning of time mankind has searched endlessly for answers to the age-old question, Why? Why do we suffer? Why is there so much pain? And most urgently, Why me? This question has often been at the center of the search for meaning. I do not pretend to have discovered all the answers, but I have found some truths that have brought me lasting peace.

I am an avid animal lover. I especially love dogs. From the time I was a child, I have had dogs as companions. Their unconditional love and boundless enthusiasm have brought me endless joy.

A couple of years ago, I owned two Rottweilers. They were very friendly dogs—as long as I lay still. One weighed 100 pounds and the other 120 pounds. Both dogs were very affectionate and lovable, but they did three things over a short time that motivated me to take dramatic measures in their lives.

First, I came home from work one day to discover that my living room couch was in the family room. When your dogs move major pieces of furniture, that's a problem. They had destroyed a brand-new couch by tearing it to shreds. Second, I took both of my dogs on a walk one day. Before starting out, I tied both of their leashes to my wheelchair. Then they saw a cat. I felt like Ben-Hur! Needless to say, I didn't do that again. Third, though my Rottweilers may not have been very bright, they were extremely intelligent (there is a difference, you know). They figured out that I was in a wheelchair. So, anytime I got angry at them, they would run for the nearest curb, jump up on it, and smile! That really ticked me off.

To control the dogs better, I invested in a couple of shock collars. The purpose of shock collars, frankly, is to inflict pain. Now, the level of the pain can be adjusted, depending on the need, from a slight irritation to dropping them. Let me tell you, there is an appropriate time to drop a 120-pound Rottweiler. For instance, my larger dog had a personality disorder. He honestly believed that small children are hairless cats. He liked to chase them. That would definitely be an appropriate time to drop a 120-pound Rottweiler.

There are several reasons why I used shock collars. First, I wanted my dogs to associate the pain with their behavior and not with me. You see, if I had to discipline my dogs personally, I would either yell at them, swat them, or chase after them. They would then do one of several things—run from me, cower, or bite me—none of which was acceptable. By using the shock collars as a form of discipline, my dogs associated the pain or discomfort with their behavior and not with me—they assumed some big dog in the sky just hated them!

Have you ever noticed that your children are much more obedient when you are home than when you are away? That points up the second reason why the shock collars were useful. Because my dogs associated the pain with their behavior and not with me, they were much more obedient even when I was away.

The third reason I used the shock collars is that pain is a great teacher. It is not the only teacher, but it is a great one. Why? Because pain conveys only one message: "Stop doing what you're doing!" Pain does not dislike you. It isn't following you around in life. It is simply saying, "Stop doing what you are doing!" It's that simple.

Lest you misunderstand and think that I am cruel for using shock collars, let me ask you a question: When our children exhibit behavior that is inappropriate, dangerous, or just rude, isn't it often necessary, in order to correct them, to introduce some form of discomfort, even pain, into their lives? The pain can be provided in a variety of ways. We scold them—emotional pain. Or we spank them—physical pain. Or we send them to their room—isolation. Or we take away their privileges—curtail their freedom. Wouldn't you agree, as parents and teachers, that if some form of discomfort is not applied, children often never learn. Why? Because pain is a great teacher.

If you were to put your hand into a fire, what would you immediately do? Pull it out, I hope! The cause of the pain is immediately understood and the message is very clear: "Stop doing what you are doing!" Sometimes, however, the source of the pain you and I experience in our personal lives, in our relationships, in our financial lives, and in our emotions is not so evident. Failing to understand, we often continue to do the same things, over and over and over again. And we wonder why the pain never goes away.

What would happen if you left your hand in the fire for three days? The answer is obvious. You'd lose your hand. I don't mean to be morbid, but there is a significant point to be made here. When your hand is gone, will it hurt anymore? No. The wrist may be quite uncomfortable, but when the hand is gone, it will no longer hurt. The point is this: If we ignore pain long enough, it will eventually go away. But by the time it does, we may have caused permanent and lasting damage, and a new pain will enter our lives, which often is worse than the first.

How are hardened criminals created? Are they born that way? No. Criminal behavior begins with little acts of deceit, dishonesty, and theft. At first, the person may feel pangs of guilt and even remorse (pain), but if those feelings are ignored long enough, they will eventually go away, leaving the door open for more serious acts of social misconduct and crime. The scriptures describe this pattern as becoming "past feeling." When we become "past feeling" we will eventually cause permanent and lasting damage.

One day some years ago, while left to myself at home, I became hungry. I made what preparations I could as a quadriplegic to fix myself a hot meal. I fumbled around in the refrigerator, found something remotely appetizing, and stuck it into the microwave. Counting the seconds until I could satisfy my hunger, I quickly removed the steaming hot plate from the microwave and laid it on my lap. Working my way to the table, I made a couple of brief stops to get a fork and a napkin. Within a minute or two, as I lifted the hot plate to the table, I smelled something unusual. I sniffed at my food trying to detect the source. I made my way back to the kitchen to see if something was still burning there. It was then that I looked down at my lap and discovered the source of the odor—I was smelling my own burning flesh!

I quickly got my pants off to reveal serious burns on both my thighs. The wounds were ugly, but I had no sensation of pain— one of the dubious benefits of being paralyzed. Some might think that would be a great condition to be in. Imagine if we could play football without getting sore muscles. What if we could cut our finger on a knife with no discomfort? But without the sensation of

25

pain, I had done serious damage to my body. If I had enjoyed even the slightest suggestion of discomfort, I could have avoided costly medical bills and weeks of inconvenience and concern.

Pain conveys a simple message: "Stop doing what you are doing!" Without pain, we would find only misery without end.

Unfortunately, we do not always take such an intelligent approach to the pain and discomfort of our lives. All too often we react with feelings of anger, bitterness, and resentment. Though these feelings are completely natural and many times justified, they often cause us to miss the message of pain. Pain is to teach us and redirect us, not just to torment and punish. Sadly, when we do not heed the message of pain, our behavior remains unchanged, and the pain continues, causing greater and greater damage to our peace and happiness.

Ask New Questions

In his nationally best-selling book *Awaken the Giant Within,* Tony Robbins has written, "Quality questions create a quality life" (New York: Simon and Schuster, 1992, p. 180). We are constantly asking ourselves questions—usually subliminally. We may ask ourselves what time we need to get up to be ready for work in the morning. Why do I have to get up? What if I choose not to get up? What's for breakfast? Why is there no milk in the refrigerator this morning? We are constantly asking ourselves questions—that's the way the mind works.

Let's suppose for a moment that we weigh more than we want to—whatever that is. We look at ourselves in the mirror and ask,

"Why am I so overweight? Why does everything I eat turn to fat? Why don't I weigh what I want to weigh?" At this point the mind begins its search for an answer—it *must* find an answer. Finally the mind spits back, "Because you eat too much!"

That answer may not even be true. Our weight may be due to our metabolism. Perhaps, as recent studies have suggested, the cause is genetic. Suppose it is not the quantity of the food we eat but the quality. Maybe we are not exercising or we have health problems we may not be aware of. Whatever the reason, it may not be because we simply "eat too much."

I have discovered three things in this regard. First, I have learned that you cannot get an answer to a question that you have not asked. Second, perhaps the worst way to ask a question is always to begin it with the word *why.* Why? Because it will very seldom lead to a solution of the problem, and more often than not, it will make you feel worse about the conditions of your life. Third, if we learn to ask new questions, we will get new answers.

When we begin questions with *why,* it creates feelings of hopelessness and discouragement. It prevents us from learning the real lessons that the pain can communicate to us. Asking *why* can destroy peace.

A better way to ask a question is to begin it with the words *what* and *how. What* can I learn from this experience? *How* can I avoid this situation in the future? *What* could I have done differently? *What* would the Lord expect from me? *What* would Jesus do? *How* can I please him? When you ask a new question, you will always get a new answer.

27

How Do You Respond to Pain?

I have discovered from my experiences that there are three ways of responding to the pain in our lives, each of which leads to significantly different results. The first way is practiced by those I have chosen to label the Why-ners. Why-ners always ask why. Why am I always overweight? Why can't I enjoy a better relationship with my spouse? Why does God hate me? Why me? Why? Why? Why? I have found that this response to pain very seldom leads to a solution of the problem. More often than not, it only adds more pain. Unfortunately, why-ners never learn the lessons of their pain, and so the pain unavoidably continues. Why-ners never hear, "Stop doing what you are doing!" Instead they focus on what everyone else has done to hurt them. They point fingers of blame and bitterness at anything outside themselves in an attempt to answer their why's. As long as they never learn to ask new questions, they continue to be punished by the same old answers.

The second response is the one made by what I call the Harvesters. The Harvesters are people who are truly optimists. Rather than always focusing on the pain of their lives, they envision what they can do with their pain to improve the quality of their lives. These people have truly learned to make lemonade out of lemons. They are harvesters because they focus on the eventual outcome of the crop, not on the storms. That is a significantly better response than the one practiced by the Why-ners, but it still preserves more pain than we need to experience.

The third response to pain is the one I call the Birthright.

28

Birthright people believe that they have come to this earth with a purpose only they can fulfill. Because of this sense of divine purpose, their perspective on pain is broader. They understand that pain is a teacher and their friend. They know that if they are to fulfill the purpose of their lives, change is inevitable and required. When we refuse to change in this life, life will compel us to change, and that is always a more painful experience.

The birthright response calls on that same sense of purpose Viktor Frankl so eloquently discusses in his book *Man's Search for Meaning*. When we feel that sense of purpose, we find ourselves embracing pain rather than fighting it. When we adopt our birthright, we listen to our discomforts, ask new questions, and look for ways to change our lives to better align ourselves with our purpose. Faith in our birthright gives us a worthy claim on peace, no matter how strong the winds that may blow.

The Three Ps

Pain is a part of life. There is no way to avoid it. But though we may not be able to control the degree of pain in our lives, we can at the very least develop an ability to respond positively to it. In his book *Learned Optimism* (New York: Pocket Books, 1990), Dr. Martin Seligman of the University of Pennsylvania recommends three ways to avoid looking at the problems and pain of our lives. I call them the three Ps. Understanding these three Ps and discovering new ways to view our struggles can bless us with a greater measure of peace in troubled times.

The first is to avoid looking at our problems as though they are *permanent*. No problem is permanent, especially if we view life in its eternal entirety. But, it is easy to view our circumstances as though they will never change. Such an attitude creates a feeling of surrender and frustration. Satan is the one who teaches that things will never change. He uses this perception to convince us of the futility of trying to better ourselves, our circumstances, or our behavior. If we believe our condition is permanent, it comes down on us like a weight, robbing us of peace. If there is any constant in this life, it is change. As winter turns to spring, life changes—we change.

The second of the three Ps is *pervasive*. We may look at our troubles as though they permeate every area of our lives. We may see our pain as so tremendous, so all-encompassing, so pervasive, that it affects everything we do. No problem has that kind of power, unless we give it permission. No struggle is so pervasive that it will destroy every avenue of our lives, unless we want it to. Again, Satan tempts us to believe that our sins, even though properly repented of, will prevent us from ever being a good father or mother, a worthy Church member, or a faithful mate. By viewing our problems as pervasive, we invite misery and destroy any desire for effective change.

The third P is to look at our pain as though it is *personal*. We perceive that we are hurting because we are bad. We suffer because God is somehow punishing us. We are unhappy because we have never deserved to be happy. Perhaps the greatest revelation of my youth was that I was not my behavior. We can change.

30

Taking our discomforts too personally blocks our progress, our learning, and our growth. Worst of all, it destroys our peace.

The Greatest Miracle of All

Sometimes we cry out and wish that God would take away all our feelings of frustration, loneliness, fear, and rejection. I know that he can. But I also know that he loves you and me more than that.

A friend once asked me, "Art, if you could go back, if you could have flown a plane, driven with a different friend, or traveled during the day to have avoided the pain you have suffered in your life, would you?" My answer is simply no. Now, you may not understand that. But if you knew what I know, heard what I have heard, and saw what I have seen, then you would echo with me when I say, "I thank God that life is hard." Why? Because in all of the pain and frustration, loneliness and rejection, you and I learn. When we learn, we grow. And when we grow, then the greatest miracle of all happens: you and I change.

You see, of all God's creatures, large and small, that walk or crawl upon the face of this earth, only you and I are afforded the great miracle called change. We can change our behavior. We can change what we think and how we respond. You and I can change! Why? Because a long time ago, a man—a God—loved you and me enough to die for us. And because he did, change means something. As long as you and I are first willing to change, then we can call on his power to say, "Peace, be still."

31

Avoiding the Apple Syndrome

The Apple Syndrome has existed since the beginning of time. Today, however, more than ever, it has been responsible for the destruction of self-confidence, character, and eternal relationships.

To understand the Apple Syndrome, you have to go back thousands of years with me to a beautiful garden in a place called Eden. Adam and Eve had been strictly forbidden to partake of the fruit of the tree of knowledge of good and evil. For whatever reason, the time came when both the man and woman partook, and the consequences were not far behind. The Lord went to Adam and in essence asked, "Why, Adam? Why did you eat of the fruit of the tree?" And what did Adam say? "The woman! [We're taking a little poetic license here.] The woman caused me to eat." The Lord turned to Eve and asked, "Eve, why did you eat of the fruit of the tree?" Eve's response? "The serpent beguiled me."

You see, it is human nature to blame our circumstances,

condition, and behavior on people, things, and environment outside ourselves when things are difficult, trying, or tragic. The practice of blaming has become commonplace in our modern world,
even though it eventually stunts our spiritual and emotional
growth.

Our litigious society increasingly seeks to avoid difficult circumstances by pointing fingers of blame. If we join in, we ignore
the remedies for our struggles and begin to become unbalanced in
our individual lives. Struggle, difficult circumstances, and pain are
all essential to growth in this life. When we fall victim to the
Apple Syndrome by attempting to shift responsibility for our lives
to circumstances, conditions, and behavior outside ourselves, we
deny ourselves opportunities to learn, grow, and become.

As a young man, I was out driving my father's car with some
friends. I was driving a little too fast, and the roads were still wet
from an earlier rain. When I took a sharp corner, the car slid into a
curb. The impact bent both wheels on one side of the car. As I
drove the limping car home, I had just enough time to come up
with a really good story for my dad.

I raced inside the house shouting, "Dad, Dad, you're not
going to believe what just happened." (That was more prophetic
than I imagined.) I continued, "As I was driving home from
school *by myself, observing the laws of the road,* I *gently* went
around the corner, when a small child darted out into the road!
Because of the skills that you have taught me and the genetics of
my body, I managed to avoid the child, but I struck the curb and
damaged *your* car. Aren't you proud of me?"

I got the same response you might be having now. My father grinned and said, "Son, when you are ready to tell me the truth, come back and we'll talk."

I stormed off to my room thinking, "I can't believe that my own father doesn't believe his son!" Then I thought of a new story. Approaching my father again, I admitted, "You're right, Dad, I wasn't being completely honest before. There was no small child in the road. It was a little dog. But aren't they important too?" Well, he didn't buy that story either. He finally dragged the truth from me, and then he made me pay for the damage.

A few weeks later, I was driving my father's other, undamaged, car home from work. I stopped at a traffic signal—and someone rear-ended me. I was truly excited about this, because, for the first time in all my young driving experience, it really wasn't my fault! And I had the evidence to prove it.

I raced home. Perhaps too gleeful in my approach, I boldly declared to my father the circumstances surrounding his newly damaged car. My father, not changing his expression, simply stated, "Son, it's your fault."

I could not believe what I was hearing! I said, "You must not have understood what I was saying. We're not communicating. I was an innocent victim of circumstance. There was nothing I could do, no place I could go. What do you expect from me?"

Calmly, my father responded, "Son, let me ask you a few questions. Did you decide to get up this morning?"

"Yes sir, I did."

"Did you get yourself dressed, or did your mother have to do it again?" (Sarcasm intended.)

"I got myself dressed, Dad."

"That's obvious. Did you drive yourself to work, Son?"

"You know I did. You know it's too far to walk." (That's about the time you get the story about how he walked ten miles to school in the snow, uphill both ways!)

"And, Son, did you decide to stop at that light?"

"Yes sir, I did."

My father concluded, "Son, you need to take more responsibility for your life."

I didn't understand what he was trying to say. And quite frankly, I was just a little upset. But that was years ago. I began to understand what my father really meant when I broke my neck on a desert floor. While I was lying in that hospital bed, it came to me. What my father was saying was this: "Son, when you are ready and willing to take 100 percent responsibility for your life—for the conditions, circumstances, and behavior of your life—it is then and only then that you truly have the *power to change your future*." And that one simple truth saved this young man's life forever.

It would have been easy to have blamed my condition and pain on circumstances and people outside myself. I could have been angry at God. But he didn't fall asleep at the wheel, did he? And besides, he has been the giver of every good thing in my life, before and since. It would have been human nature to be bitter toward my friend who fell asleep. But it was just an accident—that's all. I could have blamed my pain on life. I have found,

36

however, that despite the circumstances of my life, it is sweet and good. Besides, I have gotten into the habit of breathing, and I kind of like it!

The truth I learned was that by pointing fingers of blame, I removed the power I had within me to learn from my experience, to make changes in my behavior, and ultimately to grow. I believe that when we are learning, growing, and changing, we are happy.

As I travel the world speaking with young and old alike, I've noticed the diminishing self-confidence people are experiencing. This lack of self-confidence translates itself into their occupations, personal relationships, and spiritual growth. They often feel an overwhelming sense of hopelessness and uncertainty about their future. I believe this has become an alarming problem because it gives us a greater tendency to lean on the Apple Syndrome.

Psychologists have taught us that self-confidence stems from perceived control. When we perceive that we control our destiny, happiness, and spiritual future, we tend to have greater confidence in ourselves and in our world. The great damage perpetrated by the Apple Syndrome is the surrendering of our perceived control.

By taking 100 percent responsibility for the conditions, circumstances, and behavior of our lives, we put ourselves back into the driver's seat. When we point fingers of blame, what we are really saying is that we have little or no control over our destiny. We are driven by the winds of fate. Unless we take 100 percent responsibility, it is impossible to look for solutions, resolve conflicts, and grow spiritually. Instead we focus on the behavior of others, stating, "When they change, then I'll change."

37

This attitude is surprisingly pervasive. How often have we found ourselves saying: *"You* make me so mad" or "If only *she* would be more supportive" or "I'll never get ahead as long as *he's* around" or "I *couldn't* help myself" or "If *they* just hadn't kept pushing me"—essentially, "The *devil* made me do it." Each of these statements puts us into a mental condition of surrendering to circumstance and resigning ourselves to fate. I believe that we have more control than that.

I do not mean to imply that outside circumstances or other people do not play a role in our lives and that some responsibility should not be laid at their feet. Certainly many factors influence the conditions we experience. But if we focus our excuses upon those factors, we feed a spirit of fear and uncertainty regarding our future.

The apostle Paul stated, "God hath not given us the spirit of fear; but of power, and of love, and of a sound mind" (2 Timothy 1:7). We live in a world that is governed by law, a world where "God is not mocked: for whatsoever a man soweth, that shall he also reap" (Galatians 6:7), a world where we are given power to act and not be acted upon (see 2 Nephi 2:13). Because of these laws, we can, as Paul declared, "come boldly unto the throne of grace" (Hebrews 4:16). That is true, eternal, self-confidence.

Jacob and Joseph, brothers of Nephi, took 100 percent responsibility for their lives when they "did magnify our office unto the Lord, taking upon us the *responsibility,* answering the sins of the people upon our own heads if we did not teach them the word of God with all diligence." By taking this stance, they found strength to do the work required: "Wherefore, by *laboring with our might* their blood might not come upon our garments" (Jacob 1:19; emphasis added).

William Ernest Henley was struck down in the prime of his life with a crippling disease. Left in a hospital and expected to die within months, he wrote this immortal poem, entitled "Invictus":

> *Out of the night that covers me,*
> *Black as the Pit from pole to pole,*
> *I thank whatever gods may be*
> *For my unconquerable soul.*
>
> *In the fell clutch of circumstance,*
> *I have not winced nor cried aloud.*
> *Under the bludgeonings of chance*
> *My head is bloody, but unbowed.*
>
> *Beyond this place of wrath and tears*
> *Looms but the horror of the shade,*
> *And yet the menace of the years*
> *Finds, and shall find me, unafraid.*
>
> *It matters not how strait the gate,*
> *How charged with punishments the scroll,*
> *I am the master of my fate;*
> *I am the captain of my soul.*

After eighteen long months, William Henley walked from that hospital.

I believe the Lord desires his children to become "masters of their fate" and "captains of their souls." By avoiding the Apple Syndrome of blaming circumstances and other people and by accepting 100 percent responsibility for our lives, we acquire the spirit of power, of love, and of a strong mind. We have confidence in the future, and we possess the power to walk boldly before the throne of God.

Santa Claus Is Coming to Town and Other Myths about Faith

I t was the night before Christmas, but all was not quiet in our house. If the mice had been making noises, we would never have heard them. A family of nine children can redefine even the noblest of Christmas traditions.

I used to start dreaming of the coming Christmas morning within hours after the clock struck midnight on New Year's Eve. I loved everything about Christmas: the smells, candy, food, trees, decorations, giving, spirit, songs, and sights. But, I especially loved the *getting* part of it. Throughout the year, I carefully compiled my list of wishes. Every television commercial uncovered a need. Toy stores were the breeding ground of creativity, and the list grew by leaps and bounds.

As Christmas drew nearer, I began to prioritize my wants. Anything I needed was immediately eliminated because providing those things was just expected—that was part of the responsibility parents had toward their children. My list had to be limited to real wants, the kind of stuff I knew I couldn't get otherwise during the coming year. I did know, however, that Santa had a budget, so I had to choose carefully the wants that I had the best chance of getting, lest my parents be forced to choose on their own. I didn't want to risk disappointment.

On Christmas Eve, my parents gathered all the children around the tree. We read the Christmas story from the scriptures and had family prayer, and then we were allowed to open one gift each. It was kind of a teaser. I am not sure why we always got so excited, though, because it was always the same present every year: new pajamas. After all, my mother wanted to make sure we looked good for Christmas morning pictures.

Sleep always came slowly on Christmas Eve. If we listened carefully, we could hear Santa Claus bumping about downstairs, wrapping the gifts and making sure everything was in its proper place. My mind often raced, "Did I specify I needed that new bike in metallic blue? Did I leave enough obvious hints that Santa would know the priority of the items on my list?"

It was a tradition that we had to go downstairs as a family. But there was a ritual that had to be observed first, I am sure mostly as a form of torture to us children. Everybody had to be cleaned, scrubbed, showered, shaved, and neatly dressed in our new pajamas before we began the spirit of getting. My mother lined up all nine children on the stairs for the cermonial picture-taking, which seemed to drag on for hours.

Finally, the moment arrived we had been waiting 364 days

for! In unison my parents shouted, "Go!" And the mad dash to the living room and the Christmas tree was on. Older children hurdled the younger ones in an effort to get there first. Seeing the room for the first time on Christmas morning was always a treat. Santa had always wrapped about half of our presents and left the other half unwrapped and scattered throughout the room. When there are nine children, that makes for a lot of gifts everywhere.

Shrieks of joy filled the room. We could not get the gifts unwrapped fast enough. Paper flew through the air. The room strobed with the flashes of the camera and the relentless plea from my mother: "Look over here now, . . . show me what you got, . . . now smile!" Flash! Flash! Flash!

Christmas was always the greatest day of the year for me as a boy, just as it is for many children. Unfortunately, I brought some of those same childhood attitudes into my relationship with God and my beliefs about the role of faith in my life. From those early Christmas memories and other experiences, I developed some erroneous beliefs about how faith works. Fortunately, through my missionary experiences, personal revelation, and gospel study, I have discovered how to counteract some common myths about faith.

Myth 1
God Is Some Kind of
Cosmic Santa Claus

In some way my childhood experiences of Christmas became a part of my relationship with God. Without meaning to, and without conscious knowledge, I related to God as though he were some kind of cosmic Santa Claus.

In Primary and at home, I was taught the fundamentals of an appropriate prayer: 1. Dear Heavenly Father . . . ; 2. I thank thee . . . ; 3. I ask thee . . . ; 4. In the name of Jesus Christ, amen.

The emphasis in those prayers always seemed to be on the "I ask thee" part. My prayers were a "to do" list for God. "Please keep me safe. Watch over me. Help me score well on my test. Keep me out of trouble. Cause my parents to show mercy on me after they find out I wrecked their car. Help Jenny fall in love with me and say yes to my invitation to the prom." And the list went on and on.

Asking for help from the Lord is appropriate, but for a long time, it was 98 percent of my prayers. I raced through the few, trite things I was grateful for in order to make sure I had plenty of time to get my full, prioritized list to the Lord, so that he could work on my demands right away. Unfortunately, such an approach to prayer and faith caused me a lot of discouragement, frustration, and mis-understanding. I had fallen victim to the myth that God's sole duty is to bring me pleasure and grant my wishes as I ask for them.

Now, if you had asked me if that was what I was doing, I would have denied it vehemently. When I am honest with myself, however, and look back over the years at that behavior, I have to confess my guilt. As I discovered the error of my ways, I began to search for a more appropriate means of communicating with my God.

The Lord has said, "And all things, whatsoever ye shall ask in prayer, believing, ye shall receive" (Matthew 21:22). I didn't have any trouble with the asking part. I had trouble with the believing part. Faith is an action verb. Faith requires that we do something. To ask God to do something, we must first be willing to do our part. Since I learned that principle, I am much more cautious about what I ask for. I first ask myself, "Am I willing to do all that is required of me?" Only after I can honestly answer that question *yes* am I ready to petition the Lord for his help.

Another habit that I have made is to spend more time expressing gratitude. My mission president taught me that, in effective leadership, I should always share at least two positive things about the individual I had a stewardship over before expressing a constructive criticism. This practice always created a better foundation for communication and improved our relationship.

In prayer, I now follow a similar pattern of spending twice as much time thanking God for his rich blessings in specific detail as I do creating my "to do" list for him. Completely aside from the fact that to express gratitude to God is a commandment, it is also an act of faith. To exercise faith is to act as if our prayers have been answered. If I truly believe that God will hear and answer my righteous desire, I will spend more time thanking rather than just asking.

When we stop treating God as though he is some kind of a cosmic Santa Claus, we will find that the nature of our prayers changes, our relationship with him improves, and our faith is strengthened. It is not God's purpose to meet our every demand but rather to provide support, love, light, and strength. By seeing

God as the great resource he is, we will stop abusing our communication with him and start asking better questions. When we ask better questions, we will get better answers.

Myth 2
God Will Deliver Us
from the Consequences
of Our Bad Choices

I was ten years old and completely bored by the sacrament meeting speakers' dissertations. Before long my mind was envisioning the G.I. Joe that I had recently received for Christmas. That G.I. Joe had a parachute strapped to his back. He also had a slingshot that could be used to shoot him high into the air, where the parachute would open and the small, plastic figure would float gently back to the earth.

Then I had my first major revelation. I thought, If G.I. Joe can do it, so can my younger brother. I dragged my little brother up to the top of our two-story house the minute we got home from church. Taking a sheet from the bed along with me, I told my brother to hold on to all four corners of the sheet and jump off the roof. He was not as enthusiastic as I was about the whole adventure, however. His refusal became more adamant as I pushed him closer to the edge.

Finally, I grabbed the sheet from him and declared that I would demonstrate how it all worked. Grabbing all four corners tightly, I jumped from the rooftop. About the time I was passing the balcony, I had my second major revelation: I wasn't going to slow down. Suddenly, I became a fervent believer in prayer. My lips moved so fast in my attempt to communicate with God that the wind caused them to whistle! The fall seemed to last an eternity. I made more promises to God during the descent than I could possibly have ever fulfilled. As you can guess, moments later I crashed to the ground at full speed.

It is easy for me now to understand that my prayer and my faith were somewhat misplaced, but at the time I was disappointed that God had not saved me. Since then, I have had other experiences in which I made inappropriate requests of God in an effort to avoid the natural consequences of my own foolish behavior. As much as Heavenly Father loves his children, it is misplaced faith that asks him to prevent all pain in this life, especially the pain we create for ourselves. My mission president taught me that it was foolish to think I could sow my wild oats on Saturday and pray for crop failure on Sunday.

Unfortunately, many of my experiences with prayer have been based on this myth. I have prayed that God would help me score well on a test that was critical to my educational future, yet I never studied for it. I have asked my Father in Heaven to bless me with good health while I was abusing my body with junk food and poor eating habits. I have petitioned him for safety and then driven faster than the posted speed limit without a seat belt on. When we ask God to remove the natural consequences of our own behavior, we set ourselves up for disappointment and frustration.

The Lord declared through Joseph Smith: "If ye are prepared ye shall not fear" (D&C 38:30). Fear is the opposite of faith. If we want to exercise real faith and eliminate fear, we must first do all we can do to prepare. I have heard of many instances in which well-intentioned Saints have taken to heart the admonition of the Lord to "neither take ye thought beforehand what ye shall say." Unfortunately, that is all too often an excuse not to prepare, and then they wonder why they experienced fear and the results of their words were less than satisfying. What these well-intentioned Saints missed was the rest of the verse, in which the Lord commands us to "treasure up in your minds continually the words of life" (D&C 84:85). In short, prepare!

Asking or expecting the Lord to help us escape the natural consequences of our behavior is contrary to the purposes of faith and will only lead to frustration in our relationship with God.

Myth 3
If God Does Not Answer Yes to Our Prayers, It's Because We Don't Have Enough Faith

Breaking my neck in a serious automobile accident was the most painful experience of my life. Every day I prayed that God would heal me and take from me the physical condition of my life. I asked him to restore me to the health I had enjoyed before the accident left me paralyzed.

After more than ten years of being in a wheelchair, I still persist in my prayers for that healing, but I have had to guard against feeling that because I have not been healed yet, I do not yet have enough faith. Though faith is a growing thing, and I believe that I

48

can always find greater measures of faith in my life, I have also had to understand that some miracles just take time.

Oscar Wilde said, "When the gods wish to punish us they answer our prayers" (*An Ideal Husband,* act 2). If God answered *yes* to all prayers, there would be no sickness, no discomfort, no death, no hunger, no pain, no adversity, no poverty, no challenges, no disappointments, and especially, no freedom. If there were no pain, there would be no learning, no growth, and no change. And without those things, why would we be here?

It is my testimony that God does love us. It is my belief that though sometimes we cry out and wish that God would remove all the pain from our lives, he loves us more than that. He loves us enough to bless us with the miracle of time. By so doing, he provides you and me with our greatest opportunities for growth and change, essential ingredients of immortality and eternal life.

God is not a cosmic Santa Claus. Faith does not remove the natural consequences of our poor decisions. And just because God does not always answer our prayers in the way we desire, that does not mean that we are devoid of faith and found wanting in the eyes of the Lord. These three myths and others often contribute to feelings of inadequacy and failure in exercising our faith. By avoiding these myths and exercising faith as God intended it to be used, we can build our relationship with him and come before his throne boldly. Faith is more than just one of the basic principles of the gospel; it is the power that will bring us safely home again.

Cast Your Bread upon the Waters, and It May Come Back Soggy

S hortly after being discharged from the hospital after nearly four months of rehabilitation, I was driving around with Dallas, running errands on a beautiful, sunny afternoon. It wasn't long before it became necessary to fill the car with gas. As we pulled up to the self-service island of a gas station, I realized I felt distraught.

Filling the car with gas was a task I had always performed for Dallas. Not only was it the gentlemanly thing to do but it was one way of showing Dallas how much I loved and appreciated her. Now, because of the obvious change in circumstances, it was necessary for Dallas to do it.

Always able to understand my emotional pain, she cheerfully jumped from the car and headed for the nearest gas pump, content that if I had been able to pump the gas, I would gladly have done it. Nearby a gentleman was filling up his own car. He glanced in

51

my direction. He looked at Dallas dutifully taking care of the needs of the car and then back again at me.

Unwilling to put the question to rest in his mind, he approached Dallas. "Do you always fill the car? Why is that guy just sitting there while you do all the work? Who does he think he is, anyway?"

Dallas's answer was simple and direct, "He's my fiancé and he's in a wheelchair." The man, embarrassed, replied, "Oh. I'm sorry."

Dallas quickly continued, "He was hurt in a car accident a few months ago. He always did this job before, and he would do it now, too, if he could. Thanks, though, for being concerned." She walked back to the car.

As we drove off, Dallas relayed the conversation that had taken place. That anguished feeling was there again, but I was glad the matter was cleared up. We talked about how easy it is for people to judge others. We discussed how "man looketh on the outward appearance, but the Lord looketh on the heart" (1 Samuel 16:7). I felt relieved, knowing that the Lord would be my ultimate judge.

Just about the time we had finished filling ourselves with an inflated sense of self-righteousness, we pulled into a food mart on the corner. We were thirsty. For obvious reasons, I stayed in the car while Dallas ran in to get our drinks. As I was waiting, a car pulled into the stall beside me. A young woman jumped out and went inside. A young man was with her, too, and I watched out of the corner of my eye. I watched the young woman pull two cold drinks from the refrigeration unit, pay for them at the front counter, and return to her car where the young man was waiting for his drink.

I couldn't believe my eyes. I was appalled. "He doesn't deserve her," I mentally criticized.

Then I realized what I had just done. I let out a hearty laugh, this time at myself. Who was I to lay that charge to his name? I knew nothing of who he was, where he had come from, or what circumstances had brought him to where he now was. Surely, I did not understand the thoughts or intents of his heart, let alone have the insight and perspective necessary to make a righteous judgment. Now, when I am tempted to lay a sin on anyone, I simply remember that day and laugh.

"Judge not, that ye be not judged" (Matthew 7:1). Most of us are very familiar with the Lord's admonition to refrain from passing judgment on other people. I am not sure, though, how many of us truly understand the consequences of that behavior and how it directly affects our peace, particularly in times of struggle.

Most of us could probably finish the Lord's passage on judgment from memory. "For with what judgment ye judge, ye shall be judged: and with what measure ye mete, it shall be measured to you again" (Matthew 7:2). It is natural to conclude from this instruction that the judgments and measures we use against others will be used on us on that great final day, when we will all stand before God to be judged of our works. That alone should be enough to motivate us to avoid judging others inappropriately but it still says nothing of the unhappiness and unrest it will bring to us here and now. I believe the warning "with what judgment ye judge, ye shall be judged: and with what measure ye mete, it shall be measured to you again" also has a much more present application.

My mission president called it the Law of the Boomerang. My friend Brent Yorgason calls it the Law of Reciprocity. In high school, I just called it painful. As a junior at Gunderson High School in San Jose, California, I had an attitude. Now, an attitude can be quite dangerous when you weigh only 145 pounds. After class one afternoon, one of the varsity football players was walking toward me from the other end of a long hallway. He was so arrogant. You could just tell by the way he walked. He always got all of the girls, too. The closer we got to each other, the more I hated him.

"I ought to deck him, just to teach him a lesson," I thought. Strong thoughts, especially since he weighed about 195 pounds and stood 6' 4", and his arms were the size of my waist. While fantasizing my conquest of the school gridiron hero, without realizing it I was staring my enemy down. Before I knew it, we were only a few feet apart and he was staring intently back. Both of us came to a stop.

"What are you staring at, runt?" He caught me off guard, but everybody was watching us, so, trying to retain some semblance of pride, I responded, "The ugliest thing I have seen all day. You!" The next few moments are not so clear. A big object that looked very much like a fist landed right on my jaw. The next thing I remember seeing was the ceiling and then lots of stars.

Ecclesiastes says, "Cast thy bread upon the waters: for thou shalt find it after many days" (Ecclesiastes 11:1). The law, whatever you want to call it, is simple: Whatever you send out will always come back. Therefore, be very careful what you send out.

It is called Deutch's Law in philosophy. Dr. Robert Deutch taught, "The more we act in a certain way the more others will act in a similar way" (in Brenton and Margaret Yorgason, *Sacred Intimacy* [Salt Lake City: Deseret Book, 1989], p. 59). When we are unkind, we can expect unkindness in return. When we are critical of others, we should expect others to be critical of us. If we gossip, we can expect others will talk about us in unflattering terms. When we frown on the world, we can expect the world to frown back at us. "With what judgment ye judge, ye shall be judged: and with what measure ye mete, it shall be measured to you again."

When we are judgmental and critical of others, they measure us in the same way. Then, when they become critical of us, we lash out to return the unkindness. What a vicious cycle of unhappiness and misery. "Cast thy bread upon the waters." Be careful what you cast.

It is easy to walk the path of bitterness and anger. It is common to lash out at others. That behavior, while natural, only perpetuates our own misery. It does nothing to stop the pain or heal the wounds. Rather, bitterness is returned for bitterness, anger for anger, and judgment for judgment.

Just Say No

I was a part of an exclusive club when I was a teenager. It was

55

our own circle of friends, and we controlled who could get in and who was left out. Our favorite activity was toilet-papering every house within the ward boundaries that had a beautiful young woman living within its walls. With toilet paper stolen from our families' two-year emergency supply, we would skillfully cover every bush, tree, shrub, and fence within reach. Quietly we worked away in the dark until the house and yard looked like Christmas in June. If we really wanted to be mischievous, we turned the sprinklers on to make the cleanup next to impossible. As you might imagine, we were well liked in our ward. As you can also guess, in accordance with the laws of boomerangs and reciprocity, and even Deutch's Law, our homes got TP'd an unusual number of times, too.

To maintain our exclusive circle, our club also identified people we considered enemies of our group. One of them was Todd. He was different. He hung out with a rough crowd. He drank and smoked. His habits were bad, so he therefore must be bad himself. Three of the four members of our little group disliked him, so we decided to exclude him and make him feel our indignation and wrath.

We had only one problem. My brother Paul said no. That was it. Despite the fact that Paul was the youngest in our tiny band of marauders, he could not be persuaded to dislike Todd. He just said no. I was infuriated. How could Paul not honor the wishes of his best friends and his brother? Paul said he felt it was wrong to be unfriendly and cruel to someone else, even if he was different. He said not only would he not consider Todd to be his enemy but he would go out of his way to befriend him. That was the last straw. That was insubordination and mutiny, and it had to be dealt with swiftly. We told Paul that if he didn't acknowledge Todd as his enemy and avoid friendly contact with him, he would be officially kicked out. How's that for motivation? Despite our threats, his answer was the same: no. We kicked him out.

I felt so guilty for what I had done to my brother that a few days later I left the club myself, and it quickly dissolved. To Paul's eternal credit, he made good on his promise to befriend Todd. Despite Paul's best efforts, however, Todd committed suicide four years later. To this day I still feel pangs of guilt—perhaps I could have done more. Would things have been different for Todd if, rather than drawing a circle to keep him out, I had found a way to bring him in? I will eventually have to answer those questions before God himself.

What I discovered is that when I drew any circle to exclude others, however justified my judgments, I built the walls of my own prison. Walls to keep others out only keep us in. Drawing lines in the sands of judgment works only to condemn ourselves. Unrighteous judgment, I believe, is a significant cause for the loss of peace in our lives, however rough or calm the seas may be.

Be careful what bread you cast. Alma had a different way of expressing this law to his son Corianton. "Therefore, my son, see that you are merciful unto your brethren; deal justly, judge righteously, and do good continually; and if ye do all these things then shall ye receive your reward; yea, ye shall have mercy restored unto you again; ye shall have justice restored unto you again; ye shall have a righteous judgment restored unto you again; and ye shall have good rewarded unto you again. For that which ye do send out shall return unto you again" (Alma 41:14-15).

The vicious cycle does have a solution. It is called love. We have a choice in this process. God has declared that we are here to act and not to be acted upon. Viktor Frankl, who suffered in Nazi concentration camps and lost nearly everything he had, declared: "And this is the freedom which we have last of all—to choose one's own way; to choose one's own attitude given any set of circumstances." He was certainly qualified to say that.

When others hate us, we can love them. When others despitefully use us, we can befriend them. When the world draws circles to keep us out, we can etch our own circles to bring them in. We can choose to respond with love. Love also reciprocates in kind. The laws of the Boomerang and Reciprocity, and even Deutch's Law, work as well with love as with hate.

When our lives are filled with stress and turmoil and the waves of life seem to be crashing in upon us, that is not the time to respond with bitterness, envy, or unrighteous judgment of others. Those responses only elicit bitterness in return and rob us of our precious peace when we need the Savior's peace the most. To judge is a poison that in the end destroys only ourselves. To spread malicious gossip only assures that the same will be done for us.

Choose differently. Choose to include rather than exclude. Choose to understand rather than close your mind. Choose to listen rather than just respond. Choose to love rather than judge, and His peace is assured.

The Search

The sun rose, warming Mathias's back as he sat reading in his garden. The sounds of the city started up as traders made their way to the marketplace for the day. A smile spread softly across Mathias's face. He lived in Jerusalem during a period of unrest and change, but he had done well as a trader himself. Now he was enjoying the benefits of the years of sacrifice and labor spent while he was young and strong. His only regret was that he had neglected to seek out a companion for his life. But now he was betrothed to Rachel, and they would be together shortly. Mathias felt truly blessed. All except for a gnawing feeling in the pit of his stomach that would not go away.

It was a spot. That was all. A small, reddish spot on the back of his leg that would not go away. At first, Mathias gave it little thought. When the wound refused to heal, it troubled his mind. He had to know. He traveled to the temple to find his boyhood friend Daniel, a priest. Daniel would know what to do.

Daniel greeted Mathias with a warm embrace. When the small talk was concluded, Mathias showed Daniel the spot that would not heal. Trying to hide his fear, Daniel invited Mathias to stay with him for a fortnight. By then they would know.

For two weeks Mathias stayed in a small, dark bedroom off the back of Daniel's modest home. Day and night Mathias read and prayed. Surely God would not punish him in this way. Mathias's life had been blessed from the beginning. God must have greater things in mind for him than this. Mathias prayed with more energy and intent than ever before in his life. Why, when his life was just beginning, was it being threatened?

Mathias knew how lepers lived. They were doomed to a slow, miserable, and lonely death. Their skin rotted until it fell off the bone. They were condemned to beg for food on the streets. They were not allowed to wander among the people. The law required that any time another person approached they must cry out, "Unclean! Unclean!" A leper's life was misery without hope. Surely there must be a prophet in Israel who could save him. But Mathias knew there had not been a prophet in Israel for centuries.

After the two weeks had passed, Daniel and Mathias knew. Daniel promised to deliver to Rachel a letter explaining Mathias's fate. The letter declared his undying love and tragic future. As Mathias was leaving, a young man rushed through the door.

"Please forgive me, Mathias. Please forgive me!" the young man begged. Mathias recognized him as Immanuel, who worked for his chief competitor in the marketplace. Mathias asked, "What have I to forgive you for?"

60

Immanuel spoke. "I have done a terrible thing. My employer has always hated you. He envied your successes and sought daily to defeat you and drive you away. When his scheming and deceit failed him, he looked for new ways to destroy you." Immanuel began to weep. Mathias urged him on.

"My employer had me give new blankets to the lepers on the outskirts of Jerusalem. Later, he commanded me to retrieve as many of them as I could. I had to do so carefully, however, to avoid becoming diseased myself. He then made a gift of the blankets to you. In time, you would receive the dreaded leprosy, and your downfall would be complete. I cannot live with what I have done. Can you ever forgive me?" Immanuel sobbed.

Mathias's face flushed with anger. With each passing second, his rage burned hotter. "I will have my revenge," Mathias boomed before running from Daniel's home toward his fate.

The weeks and months passed painfully. Mathias traveled alone. He couldn't bear to see others suffering as he was. When strangers passed him on the road, Mathias, as required by law, drew his cloak across his face and cried, "Unclean! Unclean!"

The thought that occupied Mathias's mind was how he could get close enough to his enemy to kill him. In his leprous condition he could never get inside the walls of the city. The marketplace, where his enemy spent his days, was always crowded. But his enemy couldn't stay there forever. Eventually, he would have to travel to purchase new goods from other cities and lands. Once his adversary was outside the city walls, Mathias could reach him. He could wait until then.

Finally Mathias's patience rewarded him. He saw his enemy leaving the city with his caravan. If he hurried, he could catch him before he reached the crossroads. He had waited so long for this day. Every step had been rehearsed over and over again in his mind. Success would be measured by the death of his enemy.

Mathias hurried along the highway, concealing himself in the ravines that paralleled the road. The crossroads were just ahead. Then he noticed a small band of lepers traveling in the same direction. They too appeared to be in a hurry. That was peculiar because lepers usually had no need for haste. One of them, an old man, fell in his struggle to keep up. "Please help me," he cried. Mathias helped the old man to his feet. "We must get to the highway before he passes. Please help me," the old man begged.

Mathias quickly searched the crowd for his enemy's caravan. The other lepers were now beside the road and crying aloud as with one voice, "Jesus, Master, have mercy on us." Suddenly, a man who appeared to be at the center of the crowd turned and faced the lepers. His voice was different from any Mathias had ever heard before: "Go shew yourselves unto the priests" (Luke 17:13–14). The throng enveloped him again.

The lepers began to run and shout. Mathias saw their strength improve and their backs become straight again. The man whom Mathias had helped began to walk and then to run. Tears streamed down the old man's face. Mathias too felt the healing power. The sores that covered his body began to close. His flesh felt like fire as it became new again. Realizing that he too had been made whole, Mathias ran and shouted. He was clean!

And then he stopped. Who was this man that he should make him whole again? Who was this Jesus who had power to restore his life to him again? Who was he? Mathias knew he must find out. He must return, give thanks, and worship him.

Turning, Mathias raced back toward the highway. Now clean, he pushed his way through the crowd until he reached this man called Jesus. Mathias fell on his face at his feet, thanking him and wetting his feet with his tears. Jesus gently lifted Mathias to his feet and gazed into his eyes. Never before had he felt such love and compassion. As the penetrating eyes of Christ gazed upon him, Mathias felt the hate, anger, and bitterness he had held for so long melt away. For the first time in a very long time, he had no desire for revenge.

Jesus spoke. "Were there not ten cleansed? but where are the nine? There are not found that returned to give glory to God, save this stranger" (Luke 17:17–18). Before he knew it, Mathias was outside the crowd once again. But the words kept echoing in his ears: "Were there not ten cleansed? but where are the nine?"

In modern times the Lord has declared, "In nothing doth man offend God, or against none is his wrath kindled, save those who confess not his hand in all things, and obey not his commandments" (D&C 59:21). Gratitude is not a suggestion; it is a commandment.

Being grateful is easy in the midst of abundance. When our lives are going just right, when our bills are paid and money is left over, when our children are obedient, it is easy to be grateful.

What is hard is being grateful when things aren't going so well. Who has time for gratitude when pain fills our days?

Does the Lord really expect us to be grateful when things aren't going well? He commanded us to be grateful in "all things." Does that mean we should be grateful when we reach the end of our money before the end of the month? Yes. Does that mean we should be grateful when we suffer from loneliness and depression? Yes. Does that mean we should be grateful if our employer terminates us? Absolutely. Does that seem ridiculous? There are reasons.

God does not command his children to be grateful in all things to serve his own selfish purpose but rather to bless our own lives. Learning to be grateful in all things promotes a measure of peace that we may never know otherwise. Gratitude becomes the means by which the Lord brings rich blessings into our lives. He declared, "And he who receiveth all things with thankfulness shall be made glorious; and the things of this earth shall be added unto him, even an hundred fold, yea, more" (D&C 78:19).

Being grateful in all things can bless our lives in many ways. It can restore peace to our troubled hearts in three specific ways.

Good Fruit

Someone once asked me, "How can you talk so positively about something that happened to you that is so bad?" Can good come of evil? If my accident and the experiences I have had because of it can be regarded as evil, then my answer has to be yes. Yet the Savior, during his ministry in Jerusalem, said: "Every good tree bringeth forth good fruit; but a corrupt tree bringeth forth evil fruit. A good tree cannot bring forth evil fruit, neither can a corrupt tree bring forth good fruit. . . . Wherefore by their fruits ye shall know them" (Matthew 7:17–18, 20).

I had the innocent expectation as a child that good things would always happen to me. I also thought that bad things happened only to bad people. As a teenager, I became embittered as some of the "bad" things in life began coming my way. It just wasn't fair, I thought. The whole eternal plan must be out of whack. Not until years later did I learn that only the innocent and the ignorant expect only good things to happen to them. It takes a greater understanding to comprehend that for the man or woman of Christ, good comes from *all* things. There is a difference. The apostle Paul stated the difference perfectly: "All things work together for good to them that love God" (Romans 8:28).

My question then is, If the fruits of my tree (the accident) are good—the blessings I have received, the love I have felt, the Spirit that has presided, the relationships that have been built with the Lord and those I love, the miracles I have experienced—how can the tree be evil? Too often we declare evil that which is really good. By accurately identifying more trees in our life as good, gratitude comes more easily to us.

A Thousand Reasons

Gratitude, even in hard times, encourages us to focus on the Source of all blessings. Someone has said that an ungrateful person is like a hog under a tree eating apples and never looking up

65

to see where they come from. When we keep our eyes focused on our problems, we only discover new problems.

In my travels as a professional speaker, I have had to rely on a myriad of different means to get me from airport to hotel and back again. Generally, the company I am speaking for hires a limousine to pick me up at the airport and return me when I have completed my obligations. That may seem like fun, but I still have longed for more freedom as I travel, rather than always having to rely on someone else to transport me from place to place.

At home, I drive a minivan equipped with hand controls and a ramp that permits me to roll my wheelchair directly behind the steering wheel of the van and drive from that position. It has been a miracle, and it has afforded me great freedom. But because my van won't fit in my suitcase, I am without those conveniences when I travel.

Then I heard that some major car rental companies have begun renting full-size cars equipped with hand controls for customers confined to wheelchairs. Perhaps that was the answer.

I rented my first such car in Boston, Massachusetts. I realized the first of many problems at the car rental counter. It was about five feet high, and I was only about three. I hollered, "Hello! Hello!" A face appeared over the top of the fortress and asked, "May I help you?"

"Yes," I responded. "I'd like to rent a car."

"One of *ours*?" the employee questioned.

The employee handed me a clipboard, rental agreement, and pen. I dropped them on the floor. Noticing that I lacked normal use of my hands, the employee asked, "Would you like the additional insurance?"

"Yes. Give me all of it!" I chuckled. The employee looked at me as if to say, "I am never going to see our car again!"

Keys in hand, I headed for the parking lot, where my next series of challenges began. I fumbled with the keys to unlock the door. Once the door was open, I congratulated myself on it—I had never done that before. I transferred myself into the car and got myself ready behind the wheel—I had never done that before, either. I disassembled my wheelchair and hoisted it over my body into the seat beside me—also a first. With the engine warm and my body positioned to travel, I reached for the gear shift to put the car into drive. Problem. I couldn't push the button in on the gear shifter to move it into drive. Taking my hand off the brake, I placed both hands on the gear shift. I wondered if I would be able to push the button, get the car into drive, and then get my left hand back to the brake before I hit the car in front of me. I reasoned, "Well, I got the insurance. Why not?"

Before I knew it, I was driving. I could go where I wanted to go and get there when I wanted to get there. No longer was I dependent on someone else's schedule or itinerary. I was free! Today, I rent cars in all the cities I travel to.

Years ago, it would have been easy to focus on all the things I could not do—and they were numerous. But by focusing on the things that I could do, I found that the Lord blessed me with more. Yes, before my accident there may have been ten thousand things I could do. Today I may be able to do only a thousand of them.

Nevertheless, I can choose to focus on the nine thousand things I cannot do, or I can focus on the one thousand I still can. By focusing on the one thousand and being grateful for them, I have learned to do many more.

The Mustard Seed

Being grateful, even while the waves of struggle surround us, is an act of faith. Nephi, on the sea with his family, was attacked by his two brothers, Laman and Lemuel. In their rage, they bound him and left him out in the elements for four days. Nephi said: "behold [my wrists] had swollen exceedingly; and also mine ankles were much swollen, and great was the soreness thereof. Nevertheless, I did look unto my God, and I did praise him all the day long; and I did not murmur against the Lord because of mine afflictions" (1 Nephi 18:15-16).

It takes faith to praise God while the seas rage. It takes faith to be grateful, even in the midst of pain and struggle. It takes faith to thank the Giver of all good things when our plate doesn't seem so full anymore. When we can do that, then his promises will be fulfilled: "And he who receiveth all things with thankfulness shall be made glorious; and the things of this earth shall be added unto him, even an hundred fold, yea, more" (D&C 78:19).

"Were there not ten cleansed? but where are the nine?" Are you one of them? Is there some blessing you have received for which you have not returned to give thanks? Are you focusing on the leprosy of your life or on the blessings God grants you every day? Return and give glory to God, and his peace will follow.

The Power of Incrementalism

T he sun was already climbing quickly into the sky. With it came the heat. It was summer in Utah, and the day's temperature would break one hundred degrees. My breathing became more and more labored as I raced toward the mountain that towered before me.

Years earlier, I had been told by my doctors that I would never again participate in any athletic activity or competitive sport. The doctors had many compelling reasons for their predictions. Aside from the obvious limitatations of my body, as a quadriplegic I could no longer sweat. I have to admit that has its advantages. I have probably saved a million dollars in deodorant, and I do have significantly more friends!

But the inability to sweat has its disadvantages, too. Without sweat, the body cannot cool itself. If I push myself too hard, or too long, or if the outside temperature gets too high, then my body temperature steadily rises. Before long, my head becomes light, my breathing becomes heavy, and my muscles fatigue very quickly. Those are the first signs of heatstroke, and if you do not curtail your activities, sometimes it can even be fatal.

Now, I was pushing that warning to its limit. For three years I had trained for a race longer than any race I had ever entered. In fact, I had trained to race a distance that would be farther than any quadriplegic at my level of ability had ever attempted. On 2 July 1993, I began that race in downtown Salt Lake City, Utah, intending to finish in St. George, a distance of 325 miles. My goal? To complete the ultramarathon in seven days—if I could complete it.

I was averaging nearly fifty miles a day by the third day. My hands were so bloody and swollen that my doctor asked me to consider stopping the race before I did any permanent damage. I kept thinking, It can't get any harder than this. Surely it will get better.

The fourth day, I faced headwinds of between ten and fifteen miles per hour and had little opportunity to rest. The winds were so stiff sometimes that I had to push even going downhill to keep my speed up. My hands throbbed and ached with every stroke. I kept thinking: it will get better. It can't get any harder than this, surely.

The fifth day, temperatures reached 105 degrees, and I was racing on a jet black road surface. I baked in the heat. My family, who traveled with me as my road crew, doused me with ice water time and time again to keep my body temperature down. My body ached, my muscles were beyond fatigue, and my breathing was labored at best. For three hours I didn't have the strength to speak

70

to anyone. I put my head down and just kept pushing forward. Each minute I asked myself if I could survive the next minute of pushing.

My head became so light that for a time I wasn't sure where I was. With my eyes closed, I focused on the sounds and patterns of my breathing to give me a rhythm to hold to. The sounds of my breathing became mixed with the sounds of someone walking briskly next to me. Assuming that a member of my family had joined me as a source of support, I kept my eyes closed. The walking persisted. With each push, I gained a greater sense of peace. Things would be all right.

I opened my eyes to thank whoever it was for the support. The horizon stretched beside me, but nobody was there. I looked over my shoulder. The nearest person to me was my sister Beverly, on a bike some thirty yards behind me. The sound of footsteps stopped as abruptly as they had come. But whoever had come to walk that hot and difficult road with me had left me with a peace that persisted until the end.

The sixth day was the most difficult. With temperatures still breaking one hundred degrees, I came to the base of a mountain that seemed to go up forever. As the road got steeper, I slowed down to a crawl. If I raised my head off my knees more than an inch, my front wheel rose off the surface of the road. Then, as I strained against the push ring, my glove slipped, and I immediately began to roll backward. I reached quickly for the brake on the front wheel. With my front wheel locked, however, and with no weight over my front wheel, my wheelchair skidded across the road as I rolled backwards. If I grabbed for my push rings, I would flip over backwards. I was headed for a deep ravine when Beverly grabbed my chair, stopping its backward descent.

I inched my way up that mountain for eight hours and covered twelve miles. The road climbed to nearly eight thousand feet before I began the welcome descent. The last fifty miles passed quickly. I could smell the finish line. Seven days after I left Salt Lake City, I rolled the final miles into St. George. Police had stopped traffic, and people lined the streets as I raced by. Tears fell from my eyes. I had made it—I had done the impossible.

We live in an instant world—a world of instant soup and instant oatmeal. We live in a world of instant love and instant wealth—it's called the lottery. We live in a world of space shuttles, fax machines, and satellite transmissions where the operative word in business is *now* and today is too late. Young people often think that by the time they are twenty-eight years old, if they don't make as much as their fathers, live in a bigger house, and drive a faster car, they are failures. Why? Because we live in a world that teaches us that if we can't have it now, do it now, or enjoy it now, then it must not be worth very much.

That's a lie—a lie that is taught by the voice of Satan himself. The truth is, perhaps the greatest things of value in life come only after great effort, hard work, and just as important, time. President Spencer W. Kimball said, "There are infinitely more [miracles] today than in any age and just as wondrous" (*New Era,* Oct. 1981, p. 48). Then where have they all gone? And why do you and I sometimes seem to miss them? Elder Boyd K. Packer said, "Some

72

of us think a miracle is a miracle only if it happens instantly, but," and this is the important part, "miracles can grow slowly. And patience and faith can compel things to happen that otherwise never would have come to pass" (*Ensign,* Feb. 1972, p. 71).

Some Miracles Take Time

What is a miracle, anyway? If you and I went back thousands of years to see a man stand beside a large body of water and raise his arms in the air, see the water part to the right and to the left, and watch two million people cross on dry ground, would we call that a miracle? I think we'd answer, Yes. What if we saw a man call down fire from heaven to consume a worthy sacrifice? Would we call that a miracle? We'd say, Absolutely. What if we went back to the meridian of time and saw the Man among men, the King of kings, our Lord of lords—and we watched him as he laid his hands upon the sick, and they were healed; the deaf, and they heard; the lame, and they walked? Were those miracles? I think we'd answer with a resounding Yes.

Is it a miracle when a small caterpillar grows and becomes a beautiful butterfly? Is it a miracle when an ugly duckling matures into a beautiful swan? I think so. (I have four sisters!) And was it a miracle when a hundred and fifty years ago a fourteen-year-old boy walked from a grove of trees, having been called to establish a church that has grown to include more than nine million members? Was that a miracle? I think we'd have to say, Absolutely.

What is the difference? What's the difference between Moses parting the waters of the Red Sea and a small caterpillar growing into a beautiful butterfly? What's the difference between Elijah calling down fire from heaven and the ugly duckling maturing into a beautiful swan? And what's the difference between the Savior making the blind to see, the deaf to hear, and the lame to walk, and Joseph Smith, with his experience in a grove of trees, beginning the restoration of the gospel that is flowering into the Church we belong to today?

The difference is time.

When we are struggling and in pain, the last thing we want to hear is that some things just take time. We want instant solutions, quick fixes, and immediate help. When help doesn't come in an instant, we feel cheated, alone, and discouraged. If we do that, we miss the miracle of time itself. And when we miss the miracle of time, it works against us rather than for us.

As I reflect on the life of Joseph Smith, I am reminded that at the age of fourteen he took to the Lord his questions about which of all the churches was true. In glorious light, this young boy was told by the Savior himself that he must join none of them, but that if he remained faithful, God would through him restore the true church and kingdom once again upon the earth. The light faded, and once again the boy was alone.

How soon do you think he anticipated the return of his Lord in restoring the truth to the earth as he had promised? Tomorrow? Next week? Or perhaps even next month?

How long did young Joseph wait? Three years. Three years passed before he was visited again by a heavenly messenger of truth and light. Moroni visited him then and introduced the Book of Mormon, which was still only inscribed upon plates of gold. Moroni visited Joseph every year for four years before Joseph was allowed to receive the plates. By then seven years had passed from the time Joseph received his first vision.

Certainly nobody would argue that the fulfillment of all the prophecies concerning the Restoration would be a miracle of enormous proportions. And those events were prophesied thousands of years before. Time plays an essential role in the working of miracles.

How Long?

One constant element in all of the promises the Lord made to Joseph Smith was that he would have to wait. Everything Joseph received, it seems, he waited for.

At times, Joseph became impatient in "waiting upon the Lord," but the Lord was building a prophet as much as he was building his kingdom. When Joseph suffered in Liberty Jail for a season, he became weary of his anguish. In desperation he cried out, "O God, where art thou? And where is the pavilion that covereth thy hiding place?" His questions in this cry for help began time and again with the words, "How long . . . ?" (D&C 121:1–2).

Many times I, too, became weary in my suffering. Many times I echoed the words of the Prophet Joseph, particularly, "How long . . . ?"

But slowly, because of the things I have experienced, I came to understand the great miracles that come through the process of waiting. As I learned to "wait upon the Lord," he schooled me in what would produce happiness and joy. He provided me with tools to work with and friends and family to help along the way. I could have chosen to be bitter instead of choosing to learn; but the blessings that have already come from my experiences outweigh the pain and anguish. The miracle is in the journey perhaps even more than in the destination itself.

Faith and persistence are growing things. And in my growing, I have focused on the promises made to Joseph Smith in his darkest hour: "My son, peace be unto thy soul; thine adversity and thine afflictions shall be but a small moment; and then, if thou endure it well, God shall exalt thee on high; thou shalt triumph over all thy foes" (D&C 121:7–8).

Time can be our enemy or our friend. Much of the outcome depends on our attitude toward time and how we respond to its challenges. I have been in a wheelchair now for more than ten years. I am still seeking the miracle of walking. I believe it will yet come, but in my journey through time, I have discovered some valuable truths about how best to deal with time itself. I have been able to find a measure of peace despite my years of "waiting upon the Lord."

By the Yard It's Hard

First, I have discovered the power of incrementalism, which is simple: some of the greatest blessings of life are received in increments. Rarely do we experience "big bang" miracles in our lives. Miracles often have to be measured by gains made over days, weeks, months, and even years. Small gains accumulate, and strength grows. Think of the tiny threads of steel that make up a cable. Any one of them by itself can be broken by a child, but once interwoven a thousand times over, the threads become nearly unbreakable. If we break our dreams into smaller, more manageable increments and exercise patience as we go along, over time we can achieve much. The individual, small tasks may not be impressive, but the accumulation of them makes the miracle. Our challenge is to remain steadfastly on the path despite the distractions and discouragements along the way.

As a quadriplegic I have achieved many goals that were thought to be impossible. Some still evade me. Despite my proven ability to race hundreds of miles over rough and hot terrain, I haven't yet been able to learn how to get myself from the floor back into my wheelchair if I should fall out. As much as it is an issue of strength, it is an issue of balance.

Last year, I traveled alone to a large city in the East to speak to a client's organization. In the morning, I awoke and felt in the dark for my wheelchair. As I transferred my body from the bed to my wheelchair, the brake holding the chair in place slipped, and the chair rolled away. I lost my balance and fell to the floor in a heap.

I was in trouble and I knew it. I tried with all my strength to lift myself back into the chair, but I fell short each time. I struggled to pull myself up into the bed again, but I could not. My mind searched for solutions.

I thought about calling the bellman downstairs and asking him to come and assist me. I wasn't sure what you tip a bellman for lifting a person in contrast to a suitcase, and besides, the telephone was well out of my reach. I had to think of something else, or I would miss my appointment to speak to an audience of a thousand people.

The sun, which was beginning to rise, started to illuminate the room. Across the room was a sofa couch. Suddenly I had an idea. I dragged myself across the floor toward the couch, pulling my wheelchair along behind me. When I got to the couch, I pulled off one cushion and placed it on the floor. The cushion was about six inches high. That was easy—I could lift myself onto the cushion on the floor. Once I was on top of the cushion, it was only about eight more inches to the top of the sofa's box spring. I could do that. Once on top of the box spring, it was only another six inches to the top of the cushion still on the couch. It was working! From there, it was only six inches up to get back into my wheelchair. I had done it!

Incrementalism works. We can achieve our goals if we break them down into smaller, more manageable steps. Too often we see only the problem looming ominously before us and have difficulty in creatively reducing it to pieces we can deal with. By the yard, it's hard; by the inch, it's a cinch.

Adding the Daily Drops

The second truth I have discovered about the power of incrementalism is how important it is to be patient and to be satisfied to grow slowly, one day at a time. In the scriptures we read about the ten virgins who were called at the last minute to a wedding of great importance. Five of the virgins had sufficient oil to keep their lamps lit, but the other five virgins had not sufficiently prepared.

As I have read and reread the account, I have wondered why the solution wasn't simpler. In the attitude of Christian concern, why couldn't the five wise virgins simply have shared their oil with the five foolish ones? A friend who traveled to Israel brought me back the answer. She brought me a replica of the lamps used in Christ's day. I was amazed to see how small the lamps were. They fit comfortably into the palm of your hand. The reservoirs for oil were so small that they held only enough oil for one. The light that came from the lamp was also just enough for one. Even if the five wise virgins had wanted to share their oil with the foolish virgins, it would have been impossible—there simply wasn't enough oil for all of them. Each had to depend on her own, personal preparation.

The same is true of us. As children, we depend on our parents to provide us with sufficient spiritual oil to light our paths. There comes a time, however, when we must find our own source of oil to fill our lamps. I have discovered that filling my own spiritual lamp is a daily thing. My reservoir is small, and filling it is not something that can be done at a local gas station. It must be added a drop at a time at regular and frequent intervals.

For me, those drops of spiritual oil are produced by reading the scriptures and praying every day. They are generated as I spend time with my family and perform acts of kindness to others. Spiritual oil is accumulated by attending church meetings and paying a generous fast offering. Oil is added to my lamp when I am diligent in performing my responsibilities as a father, husband, priesthood holder, and member of the Church.

The time to prepare is now. The oil can be added only a drop at a time. If we wait for the darkness to come, the winds to blow and the seas to rage all around us before we check the level of our oil, peace will be lost and darkness will prevail. We need to prepare a little at a time, a day at a time.

The Big Picture

Finally, we need to find patience, to understand that some miracles, dreams, and impossibilities just take time. The path to our deepest dreams and desires will always be strewn with rocks and briars—that's what makes the journey worth it. We need to keep our eyes on the goal without getting too caught up in the pain of the path.

My world-record–setting race of 325 miles required months and years of training to accomplish. As I got closer to the date I was to begin the race, my training intensified. I did much of my training at a middle school that had a circular service road nearly one mile long. On an average training day I circled the track ten to thirty times.

One particular day, my training was going well. I felt strong and aggressive. My speeds were increasing and my strokes becoming more fluid. Wheeling along about fifteen miles per hour, I came quickly around a bend. Some activity on the road ahead temporarily distracted my attention from the road surface in front of me. Before I knew it my racing wheelchair had slammed into a curb, flown into the air, and turned sideways. Still in my chair, I came crashing to the ground and slid for several yards across the asphalt road. Only my helmet saved me from a head injury. My arms and elbows were raw and bloody. Bystanders ran to lift me and my chair back to the proper position. My training was finished for the day.

It would have been easy to have become discouraged about my injuries and stop my training then. I knew when I began that my training would be filled with bumps and bruises, but I was training for something that had rewards that would far outweigh the pain.

Pain does not automatically mean that happiness is gone and peace is destroyed. If we can realize the value of time in the growth of miracles, take the responsibility of adding drops of oil to our reservoirs daily, and keep our eyes on the goal, having faith that the Lord will reward our efforts, then peace can be restored and miracles will occur.

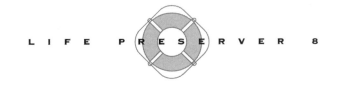

L I F E   P R E S E R V E R   8

Lose Your Life

As a young man, I was eager to serve a mission for the Lord. I idolized the missionaries and wanted to become just like them. As a deacon I begged my parents to buy me a three-piece black suit for passing the sacrament on Sunday—I wanted to look like a missionary, talk like a missionary, and be a missionary.

After years of preparation and waiting, I eagerly turned my papers in. The next few weeks were filled with wondering where in all the world the Lord would send me. I had a friend who had gone to Japan, a brother who served in Korea, another in Alaska, and a friend in Hawaii (he is still trying to convince me he worked!). Going overseas sounded glamorous and exotic, but there were also many places right here in the States where I would have loved to have served. Because most of my relatives lived east of the Mississippi and I had grown up in California, we had

83

often driven across the country. I had been in forty-two of the fifty states by the time I was nineteen.

Finally the long-awaited day came. I raced to the mailbox and gingerly carried in the prophetic call to service. While my family gathered around me I tore the envelope open. My eyes quickly scanned the letter for the place I would serve. I would be a little less than honest if I didn't confess being somewhat disappointed to read that I would be spending the next two years of my life in North and South Dakota.

I asked my father why, of all the states we had visited, we had never been to North or South Dakota. He smiled. "Son, when you get there, you'll know!" Well, just to set the record straight, I found my experiences in the Dakotas to be some of the most rewarding and gratifying of my life.

For the first twelve months of my mission I worked harder than I ever had. My feet ached from walking, my knuckles were red from knocking, and my voice was sore from talking. But I truly loved the Lord's work.

After a while, despite the effort I was making, I experienced an unsettling feeling of discontent. I wasn't enjoying the same Spirit, peace, and joy that I had been richly blessed with during the previous months of my mission. I worried that perhaps I wasn't working hard enough, and so I doubled my efforts. When the discontented feeling persisted, I thought perhaps I wasn't praying earnestly enough, and so I stayed on my knees longer. When the peace still did not return, I feared that I was unworthy, and so I repented with all the energy of my heart. Nothing seemed to help.

It seemed that the harder I tried, the further away I was getting from the peace and serenity I longed for and had once enjoyed.

Then I was sent a new companion. From our first day together, there were problems. He complained about everything. It was too hot; it was too cold. His feet hurt; he was tired. He hated his hair. He disliked his family. He wished he had been sent to a different mission. About that time I was wishing the same thing.

I could hardly stand it. His poor attitude hung like a dark cloud over everything we did. How was I ever going to find the peace I felt was missing with this missionary around? Finally, when I couldn't take it any longer, I lashed out. For a full twenty minutes I gave him everything I had. Every frustration that had been building in me exploded. I was sick and tired of his complaining, and I just wasn't going to take it anymore.

In the midst of my tirade, I noticed he was crying. My heart ached. I felt incredibly guilty about everything I had said. Gently, I put my arm around his shoulders, and immediately his sobbing intensified. There we were, standing in the middle of a sidewalk somewhere in South Dakota on a sunny afternoon, and I was trying to comfort and console a young man who was obviously hurting very deeply. Back at our apartment, we talked for many hours. We talked about his home life and his family. We discussed his reasons for serving a mission. We explored how he truly felt about himself and his progress. In the course of our discussion, he confessed that he had contemplated suicide several times, even while in the mission field. He had some deep pain.

That night as I prepared for bed, I stayed on my knees longer than usual. I implored God's blessings upon my companion in his hour of pain and struggle. In the morning when I arose, my first thoughts were of my companion. Again, I slipped from my bed onto the cold floor and prayed for the Spirit and for wisdom in my relationship with my companion. During our studies together that morning, we talked about things we could do together to help heal his wounds that were festering. As we worked together during the day, I spent a lot more time listening and offering assurance and understanding.

I became lost in my desires to help my companion. The bonds of our relationship grew stronger each day. I watched his self-esteem improve. He seemed to be getting happier. He complained less frequently and even succumbed to an occasional smile. He dressed more neatly, walked a little taller, and spoke with increasing confidence and self-assurance.

The time passed too quickly, and before we knew it, he was being transferred to another city. Our good-bye was tearful. Tomorrow a new chapter would begin, but for today, I was happy. I am not sure when or how it came, but the peace I had been seeking so unsuccessfully was back. My heart was full.

While in Cæsarea Philippi, Jesus was teaching his disciples. Peter, in his enthusiasm, rebuked the Savior for prophesying his own betrayal and death. Christ answered by expressing his desire that his disciples truly follow him: "If any man will come after me, let him deny himself, and take up his cross, and follow me.

86

For whosoever will save his life shall lose it: and whosoever will lose his life for my sake shall find it" (Matthew 16:24–25).

Jesus may have been referring to how we qualify for eternal life, but his teaching applies to what we do here and now. Attempting to find peace in my life, I had been so consumed by my own needs that I became blind to those of others close to me. My selfishness had robbed me of a listening ear, an understanding mind, and a heart filled with compassion. Desperately trying to save *my* life, I was slowly losing it. When I finally lost myself in serving the needs of someone else, I found myself again.

When we are discouraged and frustrated, it is unnatural to think of anyone other than ourselves. We become so self-absorbed, so wrapped up in our attempts to solve our own crises, that we simply do not have the time or energy to consider the needs of others. Because of our obligations to others, we are often forced to meet some minimum level of consideration for them, but we are often left feeling hollow and restless.

There is a paradox in the Lord's message of losing ourselves. It says we have to give in order to get. Doing so requires a different kind of faith and mind-set. Our thinking cannot be limited. It is not natural to think of others and be concerned about them, but, the rewards of doing just that are great.

Scarcity Versus Abundance Mentality

Before my mission I worked at a junior high school as a custodial supervisor. My pay was low, and I had a growing concern. I had not saved enough money, and there was a large zero in my mission bank account. I was desperate. No matter how many hours I worked, how little I spent, or how much I saved, I just was not going to have enough money to meet my mission needs. I spent hours going over the numbers, trying to find a way to save enough before my nineteenth birthday. With calculator in hand, I finally found a way to make it work—I just had to stop paying my tithing!

I reasoned that every penny was being set aside anyway so I could serve the Lord on a mission. Surely the Lord knew enough mathematics to know that I needed to keep that extra 10 percent just to make ends meet. If there ever was justifiable cause for not paying tithing, I had figured it out. Still, not quite sure I had stumbled upon the right answer, I took the matter to my bishop. He listened carefully to all of my reasons and calculations. In the end, he smiled and said, "Nice try, Art. Pay your tithing. It will work out."

Still wondering *how* it would work out, I obeyed his counsel. I put away most of my meager income toward my mission and gave 10 percent to the Lord. I sure hoped the Lord had a plan, because the way I was heading, it just wasn't going to work.

Three weeks after receiving the bishop's counsel, I picked up my paycheck. I was amazed to see a much higher amount than I was used to. I grabbed my trusty calculator and did the numbers over and over again. It didn't add up—they had paid me too much. I mentioned the mistake to several of my senior co-workers who advised me to cash the check as quickly as possible and not to ask questions. Admittedly, I entertained that thought briefly.

I thought, Maybe this is the Lord's answer to my problem. But I couldn't justify God's stealing money for me to go on a mission. And so I did what I knew was right. I went to the office where payroll checks were handled and told them I had a problem with my paycheck. The administrator asked, "How much are you short?"

"I am not short—you paid me too much," I replied. He stared in disbelief. "It's right here," I pointed out. "You paid me way too much money for this time period."

Still obviously in shock, the administrator walked slowly to his filing cabinet. He fumbled through the files until he found the one with my name and employee number. He read the enclosed documents carefully.

"Nope, I am afraid you're just gonna have to keep that money, Art. According to my files, you have received a raise. You must be doing something right, because by the looks of it, you were given a 56 percent increase. Congratulations."

My heart soared. There was no question in my mind who had given me that raise—it was the Lord. I learned a great truth from that experience. It wasn't just about the importance of paying tithing. It was much deeper. It was about being willing to give when there is little left to give. It was about the faith of abundance.

There are two kinds of thinking: abundance thinking and scarcity thinking. Scarcity thinking believes that resources are limited and when they are gone, they are gone forever. Scarcity thinking clings to every possession for fear that it will be lost.

Scarcity thinking values things above people. Scarcity thinking believes that if there is only one pie in the world and you have more of it than I do, it must be because you took it from me. Scarcity thinking believes that if I am ever to have more pie, I must find a way to take it from you. Scarcity thinking in governmental form is communism. Communism believes that there are only so many resources and the people as a whole are not intelligent enough to manage those resources. Therefore, the government must manage for them.

Abundance thinking, on the other hand, believes that there is enough and to spare. It believes that resources are unlimited. Abundance thinking isn't interested in taking away a piece of your pie; it creates more pies. It spends little time hoarding its possessions because there are more where they came from. Abundance thinking values people and ideas, not things. Abundance thinking freely gives and shares because there is a never-ending supply of resources—we just need new ideas to make them work. Abundance thinking, in its political form, is individualism. Moral individualism contends that there are unlimited resources from which to draw our wealth and that people who have freedom and choice will perpetuate the abundance.

Whichever is truth is up to you to decide for yourself. There is no doubt, however, that scarcity thinking creates scarcity and that abundance thinking creates abundance. Communism has eaten itself to death, and the free nations continue to share their wealth and resources with the world.

When we find ourselves in a spiritual or emotional drought, it is natural to hoard as much water as possible—who knows when the next comforting rain will come? In times of emotional or spiritual drought, we unfortunately slip into scarcity thinking. We believe that we have nothing to give, so we hold tightly to what we have. This kind of thinking extends beyond our material possessions to include our time and emotions. When we shut off the valve that stops the flow of giving from our lives, we shut ourselves off from the very blessings that return to us through the same valve.

In contrast, when we have little but still find ways to give, our giving is an act of faith based on abundance thinking. It is a faith that holds to the truth that from whence came our previous blessings will eventually come more. When we open wide the valve of giving, we create more room for the blessings of service to flow back to us again.

If peace is what you are looking for, and discouragement and frustration are all you are receiving, try a new way. Stop holding and start giving. Quit hoarding and begin sharing. Lose your life for the Savior's sake, and his peace will be your reward.

Learning to Laugh Again

A few years ago, my family convinced me that it was in my best interest to learn how to scuba dive with them in Hawaii. Feeling up to the adventure, I agreed.

I went through all of the safety instruction, training, and education beside a hotel pool. Finally, the time came to dive into the ocean. With some help, I struggled into my wet suit. I put the weight belt around my waist, the air tank on my back, and the buoyancy compensator vest across my chest. They even put the flippers on my feet—I'm not sure why I needed the flippers, but they said it looked right.

My brothers dragged me into the ocean. Then I overheard one of them say I looked a lot like shark bait, and I suddenly got a much better idea why I had been invited.

The bouyancy compensator vest was full, and I was floating on the surface. I was relaxed. I was comfortable. It was like lying on a very big waterbed with the ocean surface rolling back and forth.

Unfortunately, the instructor had a different idea in mind for me. He swam over and let all the air out of my vest. Suddenly I began to sink. There was a problem in my descent, however. With the flippers on my feet, my feet floated better than my head. I was descending headfirst! I dropped fifty feet to the bottom and hit my head on a rock on the ocean floor. My flippers were sticking straight up. Even the fish were looking at me strangely.

The instructor, now sympathetic to my plight, swam down and reinflated my vest. Now, I don't know what he thought I was going to do, but I went straight back up again—feet first! I passed my family on my way to the top, and my feet surfaced as if they were in a scene from *The Hunt for Red October*. The instructor, who must have thought he was an engineer, attempted another solution. He thought that if he took the weight belt off my waist and put it around my knees, perhaps I would float more horizontally. Brilliant man. It would have worked, too, if the weight belt hadn't slipped down around my ankles. Now I sank back down to the bottom of the ocean. Only now I was *standing* on the bottom of the ocean, waving in the current like kelp.

My family was compassionate. From time to time they returned. They picked me up off my rock and moved me to a new one. I am pretty sure they were using me as some kind of a marker.

The Lord has said there is "a time to weep, and a time to laugh; a time to mourn, and a time to dance" (Ecclesiastes 3:4).

In our busy world of responsibilities, ambition, and duty, it is easy to forget that there is a time to laugh, especially when we are caught in the tide of our own struggles and discomfort. When we are stressed we tend to find little to be jovial about.

As schoolchildren we were often warned to "wipe that smile off your face" or reminded to "buckle down." Many of us dutifully carried those messages into our adult lives, valuing solemnity more than humor and straight faces more than light-heartedness. But a good sense of humor has a place in our busy lives.

Joan Griffith wrote: "Have you ever felt stressed out? That hope, joy, and peace are long-lost cousins? In quiet desperation you plan an escape—a night with the VCR watching stupid comedies. You are consumed by belly laughs. The grin lingers. In the morning your bounce is back and that old creative energy soars freely again. Was this merely an attitude fix, or did your physiology improve?" (*Omni,* Aug. 1992, p. 18).

Laughter provides many physiological, emotional, and spiritual benefits. A group of Swedish medical researchers concluded that laughter helps the body generate its own medication. Norman Cousins, in his best-selling book *Anatomy of an Illness,* reported that "ten minutes of solid belly laughter would give me two hours of pain-free sleep." Because his illness involved severe inflammation of the spine and joints, it caused excruciating pain even to turn over in bed. Clearly, laughter contributes to good health. Scientific evidence is accumulating to support the biblical axiom, "A merry heart doeth good like a medicine" (Proverbs 17:22).

Laughter also eases the pain and frustrations of our stress-filled lives. Dr. Annette Goodheart, a psychologist in Santa Barbara, California, found that humor helps an individual to confront personal problems in a more relaxed and creative state. A study at the University of Waterloo in Ontario, Canada, revealed that those who value humor the most were also most capable of coping with tensions and severe personal problems. A further study showed that those who had the greatest ability to produce humor on demand were also best able to counteract the negative emotional effects of stress.

A good sense of humor is invaluable in the workplace. In a 1985 survey, eighty-four of one hundred personnel directors and vice presidents from a thousand of the nation's largest corporations agreed that: "people with a sense of humor do better at their jobs than those who have little or no sense of humor." The survey concluded that people with a sense of humor tend to be more creative, less rigid, and more willing to consider and embrace new ideas and methods.

There is also a "time to laugh" in our homes and families. Nancy Samalin wrote: "A not so funny thing happens to a lot of people when they become parents. They start to take themselves too seriously. Maybe it's an occupational hazard; after all, it's hard to see humor in spilled cornflakes, forgotten mittens, and crayons that have been ground into the carpet. And it's not easy to be funny when you ask someone for the eighteenth time to brush his teeth or get ready for preschool. In fact, one of the more difficult parts of being a parent is that you must constantly get small (and very determined) people to do what they don't want to do. Sometimes it seems that the job of being a parent is so much work, you can forget to have fun." Nancy Samalin concluded, "Lightening up can actually achieve better results with children than a grimly determined approach" (*Parent's Magazine,* Sept. 1993, p. 173).

A good sense of humor can go a long way in marriage and relationships, too. In a survey of thirty family therapists, Fred Piercy, a professor of family therapy at Purdue University found that nearly all used humor to halt fights in their own marriages. "Laughter diverts attention from anger and negative feelings," he says. Used correctly, it can actually bring arguing spouses together. Dr. Redford B. Williams Jr., professor of psychiatry at Duke University Medical Center, said, "Being angry is bad for your health." His preventative prescription: "It's hard to be angry when you're laughing." In other words, a couple who laughs, lasts.

A healthy dose of laughter is good for the soul. Julius Segal wrote: "There is strong evidence that those who are able to stand back and view life's hassles as absurd rather than threatening are less prone to depression, anger, and fatigue than those who succumb to agitation and gloom" (*Parent's Magazine,* Feb. 1991, p. 183). "When you laugh at a problem, you are putting it into a new perspective—seeing its silly aspects and gaining control over it," wrote psychologists Carol Wade and Carol Tarvis in *Psychology* (New York: Harper & Row).

I Am the Serious One!

More than a year after leaving the hospital, I began to learn how to drive again. The process was awkward and even dangerous in the beginning. The first vehicle I could drive independently was a full-sized van. I drove from a large captain's seat that I transferred to from my wheelchair. This setup provided the greatest degree of safety for me, despite its being a challenge every time I drove somewhere.

A few years later, I purchased a minivan that had been equipped for my use. It was much easier and more convenient to use. The van had a ramp to provide me access to the inside. Once inside, I simply rolled behind the steering wheel, and my chair electrically locked into place.

I was out running some errands a few weeks later when some of my teenage impulses mysteriously returned. I was stopped at a traffic light when another minivan pulled up beside me. I eyed the van and driver. His van was the same make, model, and year as the one I was driving—with one major difference: I had the superior V6, fuel-injected model, and he didn't! I began to rev my engine just a little. He glanced over at me and noticed the smirk on my face and revved his engine, too.

The light turned green, and we both accelerated. I slammed the accelerator from my hand controls to the floor, my tires chirped, and I sped through the intersection. Suddenly, my wheelchair broke free from the electric lock and immediately propelled itself straight to the back of my van. With the other driver pulling ahead and my vehicle without a driver, my van changed lanes.

Pushing against the force of the moving van, I made my way miraculously back to the steering wheel and slowly brought my vehicle to a stop. My racing days were over.

The new van was much more convenient, but it added a measure of risk: my wheelchair is not nearly as prepared to absorb the impact of an accident as a permanent captain's seat would be. In fact, the back of my wheelchair is pretty low. My only concern has been over what would happen if I should one day be rear-ended. The force of the impact would throw my body backward, and the low back on my wheelchair would be inadequate to hold me in place.

One afternoon, while waiting at another traffic light, it happened. I heard a loud crash from behind as my body jerked backward. I had been rear-ended. My head was now resting on the floor behind where I had been seated. With my wheelchair still locked in place behind the steering wheel, my knees had caught under the dash, and so I was doing a perfect backbend that would make any gymnast envious. I thought, This is great! I've always wondered what would happen in this circumstance, and now I know. I can't wait to tell Dallas!

About that time I noticed through the windows that the clouds were moving above me. Then I realized that it wasn't the clouds that were moving—it was me! With my hand off the hand-controlled brake, the van was moving slowly through the heavily traveled intersection. Cars screeched to a halt to avoid hitting my vehicle. I could just imagine what the other drivers were thinking as they saw a driverless van going through a red light. Miraculously, again, I was able to pull myself back into an upright position. People were staring at me from all directions. I smiled and waved.

I come from a family of nine children, and I am the serious one! From the time I was a child, my family has used its sense of humor to handle any crisis. I am not sure I would have survived the emotional trauma of my injuries and the complications of my new life if it hadn't been for the wit, chuckles, laughs, and good-natured humor of my family.

If You Weren't Born with It

Many people feel that a sense of humor is something you have to be born with. Being reared in a family that nurtures a sense of humor helps, but that is not a requisite to acquiring it. I am convinced that a sense of humor can be learned. When we are frustrated, discouraged, and feeling lost, finding our sense of humor can take us a long way back to the road of peace. Following are some things I have found useful to do when my own sense of humor evaded me during times of despair.

1. Give yourself permission to make mistakes. Excessive sobriety and seriousness can result from our desires to be perfect. Nancy Samalin wrote of parents: "The average, well-meaning parent has an intense desire to do everything 'right.' Thus, every issue—from potty-training to thumb-sucking to bed-wetting—can become a big deal. And sometimes you find yourself so busy being 'heavy' that you forget how to be 'light'" (*Parent's Magazine,* Sept. 1993, p. 173). It's okay to make mistakes.

2. Find the humor in your experiences. Don't you remember

your father saying, "A few years from now you'll look back on this and laugh!" You hated him for saying that, didn't you? But he was right. The only part he missed was that you don't have to wait a few years—you can find the humor right now. There really is a lot of humor in everything we do if we are just willing to find it. Joel Goodman, director of The HUMOR Project believes that "the world is full of funny things waiting to be laughed at."

3. Make humor a part of your life. Surround yourself with opportunities to laugh and chuckle. Post cartoons on your refrigerator, mirrors, and walls. Send a good joke to a friend. Rent videos that contain good, clean humor, and give yourself permission to let go and laugh. Go to a local comedy club that promotes G-rated comedians. Listen to Bill Cosby and laugh till it hurts.

4. Be more flexible. Theresa Fassihi wrote, "The new rule is that when the going gets tough, the tough get loose. Adaptability is tied to humor skills. You need humor most in times of crisis" (*Executive Female,* Nov.-Dec. 1990, p. 13). Learn to be more flexible. Drive a new way to work. Try a new recipe. Listen next time rather than defend.

5. Don't take everything personally. It is easy in relationships and in life to take what happens to us personally. Just because our children defy our authority doesn't mean they dislike us—they are simply yearning for freedom and independence. When our spouses complain to us, it doesn't always mean they think it is our fault—sometimes they just need someone who will listen. If you can learn not to take so many things personally, you'll find your sense of humor quicker.

101

6. Use humor in your communications. Want to make a fast friend? Tell her some funny stories, suggests Harvey Mindess, professor of psychology at Antioch University, who believes that laughter is the shortest distance between two people: "You can share jokes and both laugh and suddenly feel like you're friends." Says Stanford's William F. Fry, "Laughter is a very intimate kind of experience."

7. Give yourself permission to be silly once in a while. Do the unexpected sometimes. Dance in the rain again—barefoot. Sing in the shower so loudly that everyone in the house can hear. Make an angel on the freshly fallen snow. Play make-believe with your children and really get into the part.

Life is hard. There are times when seriousness and solemnity should prevail. There is a difference, I believe, between being light-minded, which the scriptures warn us against, and being light-hearted. When the storms of life rage all around us, few things can restore peace and calm faster than an appropriate use of humor.

Norman Cousins wrote: "Hope, faith, love, humor, and a strong will to live offer no promise of immortality, only proof of our uniqueness as human beings and the opportunity to experience full growth even under the grimmest circumstances. Far more real than the ticking of time is the way we open up the minutes and invest them with meaning. Death is not the ultimate tragedy in life. The ultimate tragedy is to die without discovering the possibilities of full growth" (*Good Housekeeping,* Nov. 1989, p. 92). Learn to laugh again, and peace will be yours.

The Life Preserver That Never Fails

I was miserable. Everything was going wrong in my life. I understand that in the eyes of a seventeen-year-old, every problem seems magnified; however, I really felt I had hit bottom. My ship was taking on water fast.

One night, speaking in confidence to my mother, I told her, "I feel like I am drowning." She responded, "But, Art, you're a strong swimmer."

I was failing four out of five classes in school. The principal had recently called me into his office to tell me that he was kicking me out of "his" school. If I wanted to complete my education, he demanded that I do it elsewhere. His remarks cut to my very center: "Art, you are a loser. You always have been and always will be. You will never serve a mission for your church—why would they want you? You'll never be an Eagle Scout—you haven't got what it takes. You'll never graduate from high school, and certainly not mine." With that, I was sent home.

The parents of one of my best friends called me to their home later that same day. Their remarks hurt even more. They felt I was a bad influence on their son. Their demand was simple: "Don't ever spend time with our son again."

I was hurting more deeply than I ever had before. I wanted to scream—instead, I cried like a baby. I laid my head on my pillow that night and sobbed. Mostly I was feeling sorry for myself, but I also felt a real sense of loss. I didn't know where to go or what to do. The waves were crashing in, and I felt hopeless.

Maybe I really was worthless. Maybe my principal was right—I *was* a loser. Surely God must have made a mistake in sending me to earth; how could I have possibly fought for right during the war in heaven when everything in my life seemed so wrong?

Sleep simply would not come. The tears wouldn't end. During the early morning hours, I crawled from my bed to make one final attempt to communicate with God. A part of me warned that I was unworthy to call on his name and that my desires would only be met with silence and disdain. I hesitated. But something pushed me back to my knees. Alone, and drowning in a sea of darkness, I cried with all the energy of my heart to God.

"Who am I? Do you know me? Do you love me?" My questions were fired in desperation—I had to know. Would God come down so low as to hear me?

What happened next is still difficult to describe. I wish I could say that an angel appeared in glorious fashion and answered the questions of my heart and mind. But, as you may well guess, it didn't happen that way. I wish I could tell you that a strong, powerful voice penetrated my mind and restored peace to my soul. But that didn't happen, either. Instead, I *felt* something. I wasn't sure at first what it was. It was warm. It felt like a small point of light touching the innermost part of my heart. With it came thoughts and feelings I had never had before. And what I learned on my knees that morning changed the course of my life forever.

Remember Moses' experience on the mount? He was "caught up into an exceedingly high mountain, and he saw God face to face, and he talked with him" (Moses 1:1–2). As marvelous as that was, something else about the event touches me even more. Almighty God spoke to Moses and said, among other things, "Behold, thou art my son; . . . and I have a work for thee, Moses, my son" (Moses 1:4, 6). That's how the light in my heart made me feel.

But there's more to the story. The presence of God withdrew from Moses, and in his weakness, Moses fell to the earth. As he did, Satan came tempting him, saying: "Moses, son of man, worship me." Notice that Satan's first line of attack was to reduce Moses to "son of man" (v. 12).

"Moses looked upon Satan and said: Who art thou? For behold, I am a son of God, in the similitude of His Only Begotten. . . . Get thee hence, Satan; deceive me not; for God said unto me: Thou art after the similitude of mine Only Begotten" (vv. 13, 16).

Satan in his anger ranted and raged. Moses "began to fear exceedingly; . . . he saw the bitterness of hell. Nevertheless, calling upon God, he received strength, and he commanded, saying: Depart from me, Satan, for this one God only will I worship, which is the God of glory" (v. 20).

Satan trembled and the earth shook. Moses declared, "In the name of the Only Begotten, depart hence, Satan" (v. 21).

"And it came to pass that Satan cried with a loud voice, with weeping, and wailing, and gnashing of teeth; and he departed hence, even from the presence of Moses, that he beheld him not" (v. 22).

Moses had won.

In the same way Moses received his strength to battle Satan, I found the weapons with which to effectively wage my war, too. Crying and alone, in my bed that night at age seventeen, I knew Satan had won a battle but the war was just beginning. God had taught me some of what he had taught Moses of old, and the balance of power had swung in my favor.

Foundation of Self-Esteem

Self-esteem can be defined as the value we give ourselves—how we esteem ourselves. Many popular books have touted the benefits of having a healthy self-esteem. While many of the arguments are valid and good, they often miss the mark in identifying the real source of a positive, productive self-esteem.

People get their self-esteem from a variety of sources. Some get it from their athletic prowess or good looks. Others esteem themselves for their intellectual capacity or social status. Still others find value in their pedigree or fine possessions. There is no arguing that all of these things do add value to many persons' feelings about themselves; however, none of them have a lasting effect.

When I broke my neck on a desert floor, I was left a quadriplegic. If I had depended for my self-esteem on my athletic ability or earning potential, my sense of worth would have immediately diminished. Instead, despite the trauma I experienced, my self-esteem remained intact and healthy—it was built upon a foundation that lasts. I had begun building that foundation on that early morning when I was seventeen years old.

The first and founding principle of self-esteem is the knowledge that we are God's children. We are literally his. As such, we are the natural heirs to all that he has—all powers, principalities, heights, dominions, and happiness. Some of God's first words to Moses were, "Moses, thou art my son." It was also the first principle of truth that Satan chose to attack in his efforts to destroy Moses.

The second truth is that God loves us unconditionally. There is nothing we can do that will separate us from the love of God. No act, no behavior, no circumstance will diminish God's undying love for each of us. Because that is true, he also loves you and me, regardless of our past or our present. Satan would have us believe otherwise. By so doing, he weakens our sense of self-esteem.

Third, as God told Moses thousands of years ago, He also has a work for us to do. I do not mean "us" collectively but "us" individually. Each of us was sent to earth with a purpose—a work to do. Many people travel through their entire lives and never find what it is because they never take the time to look. We were each born with a birthright—it is ours to find and keep.

As a struggling seventeen-year-old, that truth is what was taught to me through the avenue of prayer. It has served me well through some of the darkest hours of my life. Any self-esteem that is not firmly built on the truth that we are God's children, that he loves us unconditionally, and that he has a work for us to do, will eventually fail.

Our Birthright

Having a true knowledge of our divine heritage and birthright gives us strength even in our darkest hours. When all the world seems allied against us and the winds of adversity blow, a testimony that God is our father and that he has a work for us to do reassures us with the blessing of peace.

The *Titanic* sank, despite the efforts of the most brilliant men. Only one life preserver outlasts all others: Jesus Christ.

Peace, Be Still

The telephone rang. I picked it up and heard a woman sobbing. It took several minutes for her to compose herself enough to identify who she was and why she had called. Her voice was halting and broken as she recounted the events of the previous twenty-four hours.

Her son had been in an automobile accident. He was driving home from work late one night when a drunk driver came out of nowhere. The drunk driver lost control of his car, crossed the median of the highway, and slammed into her son's automobile. Her son's neck had been broken, and he had been left paralyzed from the neck down. As the story too often goes, the drunk driver was unscathed.

The mother now sat beside her son's broken and bloodied body as a respirator assisted his breathing. Where had all their hopes and dreams gone? Her son had received his mission call only a week earlier to serve in Moscow, Russia. She remembered how excited he had been, how eager he was to go and serve the Lord. And now this. She didn't know what to feel. Anger, hatred, and bitterness? Hope? Love? And what about peace?

There is very little to do in such circumstances but to listen. A tear rolled down my cheek. I had been down that road before.

This woman wanted direction. Which way to go? She felt like she was drowning. The winds were blowing as they never had before in her life. The seas crashed all about her. The tempest seemed too powerful to endure.

I visited her and her son in the hospital a few days later. We talked at greater length then. I threw them a few of the life preservers I have offered you here. Once, a long time ago, they had saved my life. I could only hope that these good people would hold to them.

With all my heart, I know that the life preservers I have thrown to you through the words on these pages are lasting and true. They have real power. Most of all, amid the waters of our lives, they will give us the power to find peace through our Savior. Peace, be still.

Index

To contact Art Berg, please write to:

Art Berg
Invictus Communications, Inc.
P. O. Box 246
Highland, UT 84003-0246

FAX: 1-800-400-0084

E-mail: 74117.332@compuserve.com